THE TEACH YOURSELF BOOKS
EDITED BY LEONARD CUTTS

SPANISH PHRASE BOOK

Rutherglen Academy.

R.A.

Third **PRIZE**

AWARDED TO

Christine Hartley

FOR

General Excellence

Class .... *IV*

.... *W. Paterson*

Rector

June 1961.

THE TEACH YOURSELF

SPANISH PHRASE
BOOK

Prepared by
W. W. TIMMS
and
M. PULGAR

THE ENGLISH UNIVERSITIES PRESS LTD
102 NEWGATE STREET
LONDON E.C.1

First printed 1954
This impression 1959

*Printed in Great Britain for the English Universities Press Limited
by Richard Clay and Company, Ltd., Bungay, Suffolk*

CONTENTS

INTRODUCTORY REMARKS

MORE and more English-speaking people are visiting Spain, but few know Spanish. For these a phrase book is essential.

This one is modelled closely on the French and German Phrase Books in the Teach Yourself series, published by the English Universities Press since the War.

Its obvious and principal aim is to help the traveller in Spain and other Spanish-speaking countries with the language and customs of the country.

Before learning the vocabularies and phrases, the reader should study carefully the chapter on Pronunciation and have regular practise pronouncing the exercises aloud.

The Grammar Section will be useful for reference, especially for those who already have a knowledge of Spanish, French or Latin grammar.

We wish to acknowledge with deep thanks the help afforded us so willingly by our many friends in Spain and England who have supplied us with some of the technical data included in the book.

W. W. T.
M. P.

PRONUNCIATION

After some thought it was decided not to include the phonetic script in this Phrase Book. Spanish is, for practical purposes, a phonetic language: it is written as it is pronounced. Once the following principles or rules of pronunciation are assimilated, the reader should be able to pronounce any word well enough to be understood by an educated Spaniard.

As the pronunciation of consonants cannot be practised without vowels, the reader is advised to leave the attempt to pronounce the practice words under the consonant and vowel sections until he has read all the sections (a), (b), (c) and (d). Then he should, with his knowledge of consonants, vowels and stress, be able to say these words. In addition gramophone records (or some friendly teacher of Spanish) will help enormously to acquire more rapidly an ear for Spanish pronunciation which is not difficult because it is so regular. English-speaking students should remember these four basic rules:

1. Keep consonants soft.
2. Keep vowels short.
3. Pronounce every syllable.
4. Stress the right syllable.[1]

Section (a) *Consonants*. As a general rule Spanish consonants are pronounced more softly than the English ones. Most of the following are certainly different from English:

b, not so strong as an English *b*: it is nearer to a *v* when it is in the middle of a word.
  Practice : be-BER, be-BI-da, SO-bre, BUS-co, ha-BLAR, ba-RA-to.

[1] The stressed syllable is printed in capital letters in these practice words.

c, this is a soft *k*, except before *e* and *i* when it is pronounced in Castilian Spanish like the English *th* in " think ". (In South America and South of Spain, this *th* becomes an *s*.)

 Practice : co-co-DRI-lo (K), CUER-po (K), CE-ro (TH), a-CE-ra (TH), Bar-ce-LO-na (TH), bi-ci-CLE-ta (TH and K).

ch, like *ch* in " church ".

 Practice : CHI-ca, mu-CHA-cho.

d, not so hard as an English *d*. Keep the tip of the tongue down, not up as in English.

 Practice : DE-do, po-DI-do, de-di-CA-do, Ma-DRID.

g, as in English, but softer and pronounced farther back in the mouth. Before an *e* and *i* it is pronounced something like a guttural *h*, or *ch* in " loch ".

 Practice : DI-go, HA-go, GOL-pe, GA-to, GEN-te, gi-GAN-te, Gi-JÓN, Gi-bral-TAR, ge-REN-te.

h, *never* pronounced.

j, called a *jota*, is always pronounced the same, viz., like *ch* in " loch " or like a guttural *h* (see *g* above).

 Practice : Ji-JO-na, Qui-JO-te, DI-jo, que-JAR-se, re-LOJ, ja-RA-be.

l, is pronounced with the tongue on the front teeth.

 Practice : LEN-gua, LIN-da, sa-LI-da, ro-SAL.

ll, is pronounced as if an *l* sound precedes a " y ", similar to the sound heard in the middle of the English word " million ". Many people, however, pronounce it as *y* in " you ".

 Practice : CA-lle, Se-VI-lla, ca-BA-llo, SE-llo, la-DRI-llo, lle-GÓ.

n, is usually pronounced with the tongue on the front teeth.

 Practice : NE-na, ne-BLI-na, can-TAN-te.

ñ, like *ny* in " canyon ".

 Practice : A-ño, Es-PA-ña, se-ña-LAR, RI-ña.

qu, like *k* (*u* following *q* is always silent).

> *Practice :* que, qui-TAR, QUIN-ce, que-MAR, bar-QUE-ro.

r, usually rolled like a Scottish *r*; especially when it is at the beginning of a phrase group, or when it is doubled.

> *Practice :* PE-ro, PE-rro, ba-RA-to, BA-rro, RO-pa, RA-to, ba-rren-DE-ro, co-RRER, In-gla-TE-rra, fe-rro-ca-RRIL.

s, always hissed (never like a *z*).

> *Practice :* RO-sa, de-SE-o, in-GLE-ses.

t, keep tongue on the teeth.

> *Practice :* te-TE-ra, ten-ta-TI-va, ten-TAR, TO-do, TO-rre, tor-TI-lla, to-tal-MEN-te.

v, between a *b* and *v*, and nearer to *b* when it is at the beginning of a phrase group or after *n*.

> *Practice :* VAS-co, Viz-CA-ya, VIS-to, gran VÍ-a (mB), tran-VÍ-a (mB), VEN-ga.

z, is like *th* (or *s* in South America and South of Spain).

> *Practice :* LÁ-piz, ZO-rro, Za-ra-GO-za, cer-VE-za.

Section (b) *Vowels and diphthongs.* The ordinary reader or tourist need only learn to pronounce five vowels, viz., *a, e, i (y), o, u*. These are pure and short vowels—when single they are never pronounced like diphthongs as in Standard Southern English, but rather like the vowels of the North though shorter. Spanish diphthongs are formed by two vowels, usually a combination of a strong one *a, e, o*, with *i* or *u*.

a, is like the *a* in " cart " but shorter.

> *Practice :* ca-ma-RA-da, pa-SA-da, ca-SA-da, Tra-fal-GAR, TA-pa, A-la, CA-ja.

e, is like *e* in " pet ", " tell ". Avoid the " Cockney " diphthong in " Daisie ".

> *Practice :* te-le-GRA-ma, TE-ma, PE-na, PA-dre, MA-dre, DE-do, be-BER, HAM-bre, GEN-te, re-pen-TI-no, de-SE-a, le-VÁN-te-se, en-ten-DER, e-le-men-TAL, en-fer-ME-ra.

i, (and *y*) as *ee* in " thee ", " eel ", " steel " but shorter.
Avoid the lax pronunciation found in the *i* of " still ",
" ship ", " fill ".

> *Practice :* SI-dra, VI-va, RI-ca, ri-QUÍ-si-ma, Ma-DRID,
> in-sis-TIR, es-cri-BIR, a-MI-ga, pri-ME-ra. *Y* when it
> means " and " is pronounced as an *i*.

o, short and pure vowel, something like *o* in " colour ".
Avoid the Standard Southern English diphthong as in
" polo ", " cocoa ", " rose "; *os*, for instance, is pronounced much nearer to the *us* in "bust" than to the
os in Standard Southern English " post ".

> *Practice :* co-lo-RA-do, TO-do, PO-co, To-LO-sa, Ma-
> NO-lo, VI-no, no-SO-tros, vo-SO-tros, QUE-so, RO-sa,
> U-nos, O-tros, PLO-mo, TO-mo, RI-co, TI-po.

u, very much like *oo* in " boo to a goose ", or " roof ", but
the sound is made farther back in the mouth. Avoid
the preceding *ee* sound found in the English " dew ",
" pew ", " beautiful ", etc. It is always silent after *q*
and in g*ue* and g*ui* unless it has a ¨ (*diéresis*).

> *Practice :* DU-ro, CU-ra, LU-na, PU-do, ma-DU-ro,
> a-GU-do, o-CU-po, MU-cho, cu-BA-no, Ú-vu-la, ÚL-ti-
> mo, MÚ-si-ca, que-MAR, gui-TA-rra, ver-GÜEN-za.

Diphthongs. These are formed when one of the strong
vowels, viz., *a, e, o*, combines with a weak vowel, viz.,
i and *u*, or when two weak vowels combine. Notice
that a diphthong is considered as one syllable.

> *Practice :* CUEN-to, PIEN-so, pai-SA-no, na-cio-NAL,
> ais-LA-do.

Section (c) *Syllables.* In correct Spanish pronunciation,
syllables must be read or spoken rather distinctly. The
practice words are already divided into syllables for you.
The general rule is that each syllable should begin, wherever
possible, with a consonant :

> e.g., co-lo-RA-do, cu-BA-no, be-BI-da, na-cio-NAL.

When there are two consonants together these are divided :

> e.g., LIN-da, GEN-te, QUIN-ce, LÁS-ti-ma, ÚL-ti-mo.

But,

(1) *ch*, *ll*, are considered as single consonants (and, in-
    cidentally, are treated as separate letters in Spanish
    dictionaries):

    e.g., PE-rro, CA-lle, mu-CHA-cha.

(2) When *l* or *r* follow a consonant the two are considered as
    a single consonant (exceptions are *lr*, *nr*, *sr*, and *rl*, *sl*,
    tl):

    e.g., la-DRI-llo, bi-ci-CLE-ta, PA-dre, In-gla-TE-rra,
        HA-blo, des-LUM-bra, al-re-de-DOR.

Section (d) *Stress and Accents.*

The stress.   This is almost as important as in English, but in
Spanish it is easy to discover where to place it.   Wherever the
stress does not fall according to the rules, it is indicated by a
written accent.

    Rule (1): If the word ends in a consonant which is
    neither *n* nor *s*, the stress falls on the last syllable.

    e.g., ha-BLAR, be-BER, es-pa-ÑOL, ho-TEL, co-mo-
        di-DAD, Ma-DRID, bri-llan-TEZ, se-ÑOR, a-
        YER, na-cio-NAL.

    Rule (2): If the word ends in a vowel, or *n* or *s*, the
    stress falls on the last but one syllable.

    e.g., HA-blo, BE-ben, es-pa-ÑO-la, ho-TE-les, se-ÑO-
        ra, sol-DA-dos, a-MI-go, LI-bro, LI-bros, cua-
        REN-ta, sa-LA-rio, VUEL-vo.

Accents.   (i) As mentioned above, an accent is placed on a
vowel when the stress is irregular.

    e.g., LÁ-piz, LÁ-pi-ces, in-GLÉS (but in-GLE-ses), co-
        no-CIÓ, ca-RÁC-ter, PÁ-li-da, bu-ZÓN (bu-ZO-
        nes), na-CIÓN (na-CIO-nes), ÓR-de-nes (but
        OR-den), des-PUÉS, es-TÁ, ha-BLÓ.

(ii) An accent is also used to separate, if necessary, two
vowels which would otherwise combine to form a diphthong.

    e.g., DÍ-as, vi-VÍ-a, ha-CÍ-a, o-ÍR.

(iii) An accent is used to distinguish words which, though spelt the same, have different meanings.

> e.g., *más* (more), *mas* (but),
> > *sé* (I know), *se* (a reflexive pronoun),
> > *éste* (this one), *este* (this, adjective).

(iv) An accent is also placed on all interrogative words. (Notice inverted question marks !)

> e.g., ¿ Qué hora es ?
> > ¿ Cómo está usted ?

Section (e) *Sinalefa and Liaison.*   In normal speech a vowel at the end of a word in a sense group usually elides with the next word if this begins with a vowel or *h* :

> e.g., *La Alhambra* is pronounced *la-LAM-bra*
> > *mi hijo* is pronounced *MI-jo*
> > *que está* is pronounced *ques-TÁ*
> > *su amigo* is pronounced *sua-MI-go*
> > *la amiga de la abuela* is pronounced *la-MI-ga-de-la-*
> > > *BUE-la*

Similarly, a consonant in the same position is carried on to the next word.

> e.g., *el hombre* is pronounced *e-LOM-bre*
> > *el español* is pronounced *e-les-pa-ÑOL*
> > *patatas a la inglesa* is pronounced *pa-TA-ta-sa-lin-*
> > > *GLE-sa*

The first set of phrases (pages 18–20) will be divided into syllables, and the sinalefa and liaison will be indicated as above.   When you have practised this you should rewrite the next set in the same way.   After that, practice will make perfect.

PASSPORT FORMALITIES

To enter Spanish territory a British subject must have at present (1954) a visa issued by the Spanish Consul in England. A tourist visa, costing about 27s. 6d. at the present moment, is valid for ninety days, and can be used for three separate visits during this period without any extra formality. The visa is stamped on the passport, which, of course, has to be sent to one of the Spanish Consulates in London and other big towns.

The Consul also issues permits for longer periods and for working on Spanish territory.

The visa has to be shown at the Spanish frontier or, if travelling by plane, you show it on arrival at the airport.

Latin American countries have their own separate arrangements, and the intending traveller should consult the Consul of the country he desires to visit.

PASSPORT FORMALITIES	TRÁMITES DE PASAPORTES
Vocabulary	**Vocabulario**
The passport	El pasaporte
The travelling document	El documento de viaje
The Home Office	El Ministerio de la Gobernación
The Embassy	La Embajada
The Consulate	El Consulado
The passport department	La sección de pasaportes
The visa	El visado
The tourist (residence) visa	El visado de turista (de residencia)
The transit visa	El visado de tránsito
The stay	La estancia
The permit to stay	El permiso de residencia
The length (period) of stay	La duración de estancia
The purpose of the journey	El objeto del viaje
The business trip	El viaje de negocios

The holiday trip	El viaje de vacaciones
Personal (family) matters	Asuntos personales (familiares)
The stamp	El sello, el timbre
The consular fees	Los derechos consulares
The passport examination	La inspección de pasaportes
The passport official	El funcionario
To get a passport	Sacar un pasaporte
To visa	Visar
To extend a visa	Prolongar un visado
To hand in a passport	Entregar un pasaporte
To renew a passport	Renovar un pasaporte
Abroad	En el extranjero

Phrases / Frases

Do foreigners need a visa to enter Spain?	¿ Necesitan los extranjeros un visado para entrar en España ?
When can I collect my passport?	¿ Cuándo puedo recoger mi pasaporte ?
Please fill in these two forms and sign them	Haga el favor de llenar estos dos formularios y fírmelos
You need two photographs for your visa	Necesita dos retratos para su visado
What is your purpose in visiting Spain?	¿ Cuál es el objeto de su viaje a España ?
How long may I stay in the country?	¿ Cuánto tiempo puedo permanecer en el país ?
Ninety days with a tourist visa	Noventa días con un visado de turista
I am travelling through Spain	Estoy recorriendo España
I need a transit visa	Necesito un visado de tránsito
You must have an entry and an exit permit	Necesita usted un permiso de entrada y otro de salida
Must I get a permit to stay (to take up work)?	¿ Necesito un permiso de residencia (de trabajo) ?
I want a tourist visa	Quisiera un visado de turista

I would like to apply for a three months' extension of this visa

Quisiera solicitar la prolongación de este visado por tres meses

You must have your passport renewed

Tiene usted que renovar su pasaporte

Your visa is valid until the 1st October

Su visado es válido hasta el primero de Octubre

Can I obtain a residence visa?

¿ Puedo conseguir un visado de residencia ?

I wish to live and work in Spain for some time, please inform me of the steps to take

Deseo residir y trabajar en España por algún tiempo ; haga el favor de indicarme las medidas que he de tomar

Is the currency allowance stated in my passport?

¿ Consta en mi pasaporte la alocación de divisas ?

The passport officials will board the train at the frontier

Los funcionarios subirán al tren en la frontera

Have your passports ready

Tengan preparados sus pasaportes

Your passport is in order

Su pasaporte está en orden

There is a stamp missing in your passport

Falta un sello en su pasaporte

Please hand in your passport, the Authorities have to examine it

Haga el favor de entregar su pasaporte ; las autoridades tienen que inspeccionarlo

Where is the British (American) Consulate?

¿ Dónde está el Consulado Británico (Americano) ?

There is only a Vice-Consul in this town

En esta ciudad hay sólo un Vice-Cónsul

What are the office hours of the passport department?

¿ Cuáles son las horas de despacho en la sección de pasaportes ?

How much does the visa cost?

¿ Cuánto tengo que abonar por el visado ?

I wish to seek employment in Spain. Could you help me?

Busco un empleo en España, ¿ me podría ayudar ?

I would like to break the journey here for twenty-four hours	Quisiera interrumpir el viaje aquí por veinticuatro horas
Do I need to report to the local police-station for a three days' stay?	¿ Tengo que presentarme en la Comisaría local para una estancia de tres días ?
Full name of passport holder	Nombre y apellido del titular
Nationality at birth (at present)	Nacionalidad al nacer (actual)
Place and date of birth	Lugar y fecha de nacimiento
Profession	Profesión
Condition (single, married, widow(er))	Estado civil (soltero/a, casado/a, viudo/a)
Description :	Descripción :
Face : colour of the eyes, nose, complexion	Rostro : color de ojos, nariz, piel
Hair	Cabello
Distinctive marks	Señas particulares
Height	Estatura
Remarks	Observaciones
Do not forget to sign with your full name	No se olvide de firmar con su nombre completo

Here is this first chapter, Passport Formalities, printed now in syllables in such a way as to illustrate the principles of Spanish pronunciation. The stressed syllables are in capitals and the sinalefa is indicated with loops ‿.

TRÁ-mi-tes de pa-sa-POR-tes

vo-ca-bu-LA-rio

el pa-sa-POR-te

el do-cu-MEN-to de BIA-je

el mi-nis-TE-rio de la go-ber-na-CIÓN

la‿em-ba-JA-da

el con-su-LA-do

la sek-CIÓN de pa-sa-POR-tes

el bi-SA-do

el bi-SA-do de tu-RIS-ta (de re-si-DEN-cia)

el bi-SA-do de TRÁN-si-to
la_es-TAN-cia
el per-MI-so de re-si-DEN-cia
la du-ra-CIÓN de_es-TAN-cia
el ob-JE-to del BIA-je
el BIA-je de ne-GO-cios
el BIA-je de ba-ca-CIO-nes
a-SUN-tos per-so-NA-les (fa-mi-LIA-res)
el SE-llo, el TIM-bre
los de-RE-chos con-su-LA-res
la_ins-pek-CIÓN de pa-sa-POR-tes
el fun-cio-NA-rio
sa-CAR un pa-sa-POR-te
bi-SAR
pro-lon-GAR un bi-SA-do
en-tre-GAR un pa-sa-POR-te
re-no-BAR un pa-sa-POR-te
en_el_eks-tran-JE-ro

FRA-ses

¿ Ne-ce-SI-tan los_eks-tran-JE-ros un bi-SA-do PA-ra en-
    TRAR en_es-PA-ña ?
¿ CUÁN-do PUE-do re-co-JER mi pa-sa-POR-te ?
A-ga_el fa-BOR de lle-NAR ES-tos dos for-mu-LA-rios_i
    FÍR-me-los
ne-ce-SI-ta dos re-TRA-tos PA-ra su bi-SA-do
¿ CUÁL_es_el_ob-JE-to de su BIA-je_a_es-PA-ña ?
¿ CUÁN-to TIEM-po PUE-do per-ma-ne-CER en_el pa-ÍS ?
no-BEN-ta DÍ-as con un bi-SA-do de tu-RIS-ta
es-TOI re-co-RRIEN-do_es-PA-ña
ne-ce-SI-to_un bi-SA-do de TRÁN-si-to
ne-ce-SI-ta_us-TED un per-MI-so de_en-TRA-da_i_O-tro de
    sa-LI-da
¿ ne-ce-SI-to_un per-MI-so de re-si-DEN-cia (de tra-BA-jo) ?
ki-SIE-ra_un bi-SA-do de tu-RIS-ta
ki-SIE-ra so-li-ci-TAR la pro-lon-ga-CIÓN de_ES-te bi-SA-do
    por tres ME-ses

TIE-ne_us-TED ke re-no-BAR su pa-sa-POR-te

su bi-SA-do_es BÁ-li-do_AS-ta_el pri-ME-ro de_ok-TU-bre

¿ PUE-do con-se-GUIR un bi-SA-do de re-si-DEN-cia ?

de-SE-o re-si-DIR i tra-ba-JAR en_es-PA-ña' por al-GÚN
     TIEM-po ; A-ga_el_fa-BOR de_in-di-CAR-me las me-
     DI-das ke e de to-MAR

¿ CONS-ta_en mi pa-sa-POR-te la_a-lo-ca-CIÓN de di-BI-sas ?

los fun-cio-NA-rios su-bi-RÁN al tren en la fron-TE-ra

TEN-gan pre-pa-RA-dos sus pa-sa-POR-tes

su pa-sa-POR-te_es-TÁ_en_OR-den

FAL-ta_un SE-llo en su pa-sa-POR-te

A-ga_el fa-BOR de_en-tre-GAR su pa-sa-POR-te ; las_au-to-
     ri-DA-des TIE-nen ke_ins-pek-cio-NAR-lo

¿ DÓN-de_es-TÁ el con-su-LA-do bri-TÁ-ni-co (a-me-ri-CA-no) ?

en_ES-ta ciu-DAD ai SÓ-lo_un vi-ce-CÓN-sul

¿ CUÁ-les son las_O-ras de des-PA-cho_en la sek-CIÓN de
     pa-sa-POR-tes ?

¿ CUÁN-to TEN-go ke_a-bo-NAR por_el bi-SA-do ?

BUS-co_un_em-PLE-o_en_es-PA-ña,   ¿ me po-DRÍ-a_a-yu-
     DAR ?

ki-SIE-ra_in-te-rrum-PIR el BIA-je_a-KÍ por bein-ti-CUA-
     tro_O-ras

¿ TEN-go ke pre-sen-TAR-me_en la co-mi-sa-RÍ-a lo-CAL PA-
     ra_U-na_es-TAN-cia de tres DI-as ?

NOM-bre_i_a-pe-LLI-do del ti-tu-LAR

na-cio-na-li-DAD al na-CER (ak-TUAL)

lu-GAR i FE-cha de na-ci-MIEN-to

pro-fe-SIÓN

es-TA-do ci-BIL (sol-TE-ro/a, ca-SA-do/a, VIU-do/a)

des-crip-CIÓN

ROS-tro : co-LOR de_O-jos, na-RIZ, PIEL

ca-BE-llo

SE-ñas par-ti-cu-LA-res

es-ta-TU-ra

ob-ser-ba-CIO-nes

no se_ol-BI-de de fir-MAR con su NOM-bre com-PLE-to

CUSTOMS

Luggage is inspected by Customs officers at the frontier where dutiable articles should be declared. The list of these articles varies from country to country and from time to time. Usually, reasonable amounts of tobacco, wines or spirits for personal consumption are admitted free, as also small gifts and anything which is not likely to be sold for profit by the traveller. It is a good idea to break the seal or even to open a bottle to prove that the wine or spirit will not be sold.

Luggage accompanying air passengers is examined by the internal revenue guards (*carabineros*) at the airport on arrival or departure.

CUSTOMS	ADUANAS
Vocabulary	Vocabulario
The (customs) duty	El derecho de aduanas
The customs regulations	El reglamento de aduanas
The customs clearance	El despacho de aduanas
The customs-house	La Aduana
The custom-Bond	El almacen de aduanas
The customs officer	El oficial de aduanas
The customs-house inspector	El vista de aduanas
The tariff	El arancel
The luggage	El equipaje
The dutiable articles	Los artículos que pagan derechos
The smuggling	El pasar de matute
The smuggler	El contrabandista
The tobacco (cigars, cigarettes)	El tabaco (los puros, los cigarrillos)
The perfume	El perfume
The liquor, spirits	Las bebidas alcohólicas, los licores
The camera	La cámara
The watch	El reloj

The customs declaration	**La declaración de aduana**
The export (import) licence	**La licencia de exportación (importación)**
The consular declaration	**La declaración consular**
The fine	**La multa**
To declare	**Declarar**
To conceal	**Ocultar**
To smuggle	**Contrabandear**
To levy duties	**Exigir los derechos de aduana**
To clear	**Despachar**
Customs-free	**Exento de pago**

Phrases	Frases
Where is the customs-house?	¿ Dónde está la Aduana ?
Please place your luggage on the counter	Hagan el favor de poner sus equipajes encima del mostrador
Here is my suitcase	Aquí está mi maleta
Please open it	Haga el favor de abrirla
Will you examine my trunk, please?	¿ Querría revisar mi baúl ?
Your turn next, have the keys ready	Usted es el próximo ; prepare las llaves
Have you anything to declare?	¿ Tiene usted algo que declarar ?
Do you carry any of the articles on this list?	¿ Lleva usted alguno de los artículos de esta lista ?
The new customs tariff comes into force on the 1st of July	El nuevo arancel entrará en vigor desde el primero de Julio
Have you any spirits, tobacco, new watches or perfumes?	¿ Lleva usted licores, tabaco, relojes nuevos o perfumes ?
I have this small bottle of perfume	Llevo este frasquito de perfume
This is free of duty	Esto no paga derechos
Is that all?	¿ Es eso todo ?
You can close your suitcase	Puede cerrar su maleta
Is my luggage passed?	¿ Han despachado mi equipaje ?

I have an import licence for these goods	Tengo una licencia de importación para estos artículos
You can take delivery of the case of liqueurs, it has been cleared	Puede hacerse cargo de la caja de licores ; ha sido despachada
Will you take this luggage to a taxi ?	¿ Querría ponerme el equipaje en un taxi ?
You are fined for not having declared these articles	Se le multa por no haber declarado estos artículos

TRAVELLING BY ROAD

On the 75,300 miles of Spanish roads there are nearly 180,000 cars with Spanish number plates. This number plate differs from the English one in that the letters and figures are black against a white background. Before the number is the initial letter (or letters) representing the Province where the car is registered ; e.g., M-53672 (Madrid), MA-4538 (Málaga), etc.

Traffic keeps to the right, and in some cities it is controlled by traffic lights as well as by traffic police (*guardias del tráfico*).

To keep an eye on the open roads are Civil Guards (*Guardias Civiles*), always in pairs, and carrying arms.

On the central plateau (*meseta*) it is possible to travel miles and miles without seeing a human being or habitation, and for this reason perhaps hitch-hikers are scarce. There is no word in Spanish for hitch-hiking, except the French, *el autostop*. In any case the nearest Spanish equivalent to "thumbing", *mandar hacer alto a un coche*, would have little success except in case of great need.

TRAVELLING BY ROAD	EL VIAJE POR CARRETERA
Vocabulary	Vocabulario
The motor-car	El auto (móvil), el coche
The coach (motor-bus)	El autocar, el autobús
The overland coach	El coche de línea

The lorry	El camión
The truck	La camioneta
The van	La camioneta de entregas
The hired car	El coche de alquiler
The cart	El carro
The two-wheeled cart	La tartana
The motor-cycle	La motocicleta
The highway, road	La carretera
The driver	El chófer, el conductor
The conductor	El cobrador
The motorist	El motorista
The (streamlined) body	La carrocería (aerodinámica)
The chassis	El armazón
The bonnet	El capó
The hood	La capota
The mudguard	El guardabarros
The wheel	La rueda
The brake	El freno
The gear-lever	La palanca de velocidades
The gear-box	La caja de velocidades
The steering-wheel	El volante
The exhaust	El escape
The battery	La batería
The accelerator	El acelerador
The carburettor	El carburador
The speedometer	El velocímetro
The self-starter	El arranque automático
The crankshaft	El cigüeñal
The lorry crane	La grúa camión
The bumper	El parachoques
The motor-horn	La bocina
The windscreen	El parabrisas
The spare parts	Las piezas de repuesto
The tools	Las herramientas
The jack	El gato
The screwdriver	El destornillador
The hammer	El martillo

The pliers	Los alicates
The repair	La reparación
The fuel	El combustible
The petrol	La gasolina
The petrol pump	El surtidor de la gasolina
The petrol station	El puesto de gasolina
The garage (for repairs)	El garaje (de reparaciones)
The speed limit	La velocidad máxima
To drive	Conducir
To overtake	Adelantar (un coche a otro)
To brake	Frenar
To slow down	Disminuir la velocidad
To step up	Embalar
To stop	Parar
To park	Aparcar
To repair	Reparar
To collide	Chocar
To run over	Atropellar
To somersault	Dar la vuelta de campana
To overturn	Volcar
To haul off, tow away	Llevar a remolque

Phrases / Frases

Are you an owner-driver?	¿ Conduce usted su coche ?
I have a touring saloon (sports car)	Tengo un coche de turismo (coche de carreras)
My car is a two-seater	Mi coche es de dos plazas
Who will drive to-day?	¿ Quién va a conducir hoy ?
Have you got your driving licence with you?	¿ Lleva consigo la licencia de conducir ?
Hadn't we better let the hood down? It is getting hot	¿ No sería mejor que bajásemos la capota ? Empieza a hacer calor
Look out for the bends, otherwise we shall skid	Cuidado con las curvas, no sea que patinemos
Did you see the traffic lights?	¿ Vió usted las señales del tráfico ?

You have to pay a fine for fast driving	Tiene que pagar una multa por exceso de velocidad
The traffic policeman has taken down our registration number	El guardia del tráfico nos ha tomado el número de la matrícula
I had a breakdown on my last journey to Madrid	He tenido una avería en mi último viaje a Madrid
We have a puncture in one of the front wheels, but I have a spare one	Una de las ruedas delanteras ha pinchado, pero llevo una rueda de repuesto
The box with the tools is under the seat	La caja de las herramientas está debajo del asiento
Shall I start the screen-wiper?	¿Quiere que ponga en marcha el limpiador del parabrisas?
Press the self-starter, please	Apriete el arranque automático, por favor
If you are going to town I can give you a lift	Si se dirige a la ciudad le puedo llevar en mi coche
Step on the gas, accelerate	Acelere la marcha
You must switch on the head-lights	Tiene usted que encender los faros
We are going down-hill (up-hill)	Vamos cuesta abajo (arriba)
I must change into second gear	Tengo que cambiar a segunda
Where can I park (my car)?	¿Dónde puedo aparcar?
The car park is over there	El parque de coches está allí enfrente
Where can I get this car repaired?	¿Dónde me repararían este coche?
There is a place for car repairs round the corner	Hay un taller de reparaciones a la vuelta de la esquina
Where is the nearest petrol station?	¿Dónde está el puesto de gasolina más próximo?
I must get my tank filled and have my tyres inflated	Necesito que me llenen el depósito y que me hinchen los neumáticos

How much are you going to charge for washing my car?	¿ Cuánto me van a cobrar por lavar el coche ?
Slow-down !	¡ Despacio !
One-way street	Dirección única
Speed limit : eighty kilometres	Velocidad máxima : ochenta kilómetros
Beware of the cross-roads !	¡ Cuidado ! Cruce de carreteras
Main road ahead	Atención : carretera principal
Street repairs	Calles en reparación
Diversion	Desviación
Level crossing	Paso a nivel

TRAVELLING BY RAIL

Of the 18,500 kilometres of track run by the Spanish Railways, 14,700 kilometres are controlled by the " RENFE " (the Spanish National Railway Network), which is an undertaking under the protection of the state. The traveller who crosses the Pyrenees can enter Spain by Canfranc, Puigcerdá, Port Bou or Irún. This latter route is the one most used by people travelling from England. The 608 kilometres between Irún and Madrid can be travelled in ordinary trains or in the " Talgo ". This is a special train which leaves Irún on Tuesdays, Thursdays and Saturdays at 9.20 a.m. and arrives in Madrid at 6.25 p.m. It consists of an articulated train where each carriage has one bogie in the middle and whose front leans on the back of the preceding carriage. It is made up of twelve carriages, each with a capacity for twelve passengers. It is the fastest train on this line ; for the express, which is the second fastest, takes twelve hours to cover the same distance.

On most of the other Spanish lines, besides the ordinary trains, there are also the " TAF " (Fiat Railcars) made up of three units with both forward and reverse traction. Their capacity is 250 travellers, and the price of a ticket is the same as that of a first-class ticket for any ordinary train.

The traveller in Spain has not only to show his ticket to get on the platform but also to have it clipped by the inspector

during the journey. Any irregularity observed by the inspector is charged to the traveller as a supplement, and he is given a receipt. Tickets are collected at the exit at the end of the journey.

At the main stations travellers are informed about the train's departure by means of loud-speakers which announce the departure time and the platform where the train is. In small stations it is enough to know that the departure of "Up" trains with even numbers (going to Madrid) is signalled by three strokes on a bell, and that the departure of " Down " trains with odd numbers (coming from Madrid) is signalled by three strokes on a bell followed by a blast on the station-master's whistle.

TRAVELLING BY RAIL — VIAJE POR FERROCARRIL

Vocabulary — Vocabulario

The transport	El transporte
The railway	El ferrocarril
The station	La estación
The train	El tren
The freight train	El (tren de) mercancías
The express train	El tren expreso, el rápido
The slow train	El tren ómnibus
The electric train	El tren eléctrico
The enquiry office	La oficina de información
The booking-office	La taquilla
The fare	El precio del billete
The ticket	El billete
The platform ticket	El billete de andén
The ticket collector	El portero
The waiting-room	La sala de espera
The canteen	La cantina
The cloak-room	El tocador
The lavatory	El lavabo, el W.C.
The left-luggage department	La consigna
The platform	El andén
The goods van	El vagón (para mercancías)

The coach, carriage	El coche (para viajeros)
The compartment	El departamento
The seat	El asiento
The corner seat by the corridor	El asiento junto al pasillo
The window seat	El asiento junto a la ventanilla
The sleeping-car	El coche-camas
The buffet, dining-car	El coche-restaurante
The engine	La locomotora
The engine-driver	El maquinista
The stoker	El fogonero
The brakeman, signal-man	El guardafreno, el guardavía
The station-master	El jefe de estación
The switchman	El guardaaguja
The ticket inspector	El interventor
The speed	La velocidad
The porter	El mozo de equipajes
The soot	El hollín
The smoke	El humo
The rails	Los carriles
The railway-sleepers	Las traviesas
The arrival	La llegada
The departure	La salida
The tunnel	El túnel
To reserve seats	Reservar asientos
To lean out of the window	Asomarse a la ventanilla
To get into the train	Subirse al tren
To get out of the train	Apearse del tren
To get out whilst the train is in motion	Apearse cuando el tren está en marcha

Phrases

Frases

Where do I get a ticket?	¿ Dónde se sacan los billetes ?
Is the booking-office open?	¿ Está abierta la taquilla ?
One third return Madrid for the 9.40 express, and a platform ticket, please	Un tercera de ida y vuelta a Madrid para el expreso de las 9.40 y un billete de andén

Are you travelling via Irún by the Talgo?	¿ Va usted por Irún en el Talgo ?
Which is the shortest way from San Sebastián to Córdoba?	¿ Cuál es el trayecto más corto entre San Sebastián y Córdoba ?
What is the fare from the frontier to Madrid?	¿ Cuánto vale el billete entre la frontera y Madrid ?
You have to pay a surcharge on your ticket	Tiene usted que pagar suplemento en su billete
Have your money ready	Tengan preparado el cambio
Can I break the journey?	¿ Podría interrumpir el viaje ?
Shall I get the connection?	¿ Cogeré la combinación en el empalme ?
Where must I change?	¿ Dónde tengo que transbordar ?
Where is the Station Hotel?	¿ Dónde está el Hotel de la Estación ?
Can you tell me if the train will be late?	¿ Podría decirme si viene retrasado el tren ?
Porter, please register this luggage to Venta de Baños	Mozo : haga el favor de facturar este equipaje hasta Venta de Baños
You will have to pay excess luggage on this trunk	Tendrá usted que pagar exceso de equipaje en este baúl
Please bring me the registration slip to the first-class coach	Haga el favor de traerme el talón al coche de primera
Please leave the suit-cases in the left-luggage department	Por favor, déjeme en consigna las maletas
From which platform does the slow train start?	¿ De qué andén sale el tren ómnibus ?
Platform No. 4 through the subway	Andén número IV, cruzando por el pasillo subterráneo
I was lucky—I got a seat near the window, my back to the engine	Tuve suerte : cogí un asiento junto a la ventanilla, de espaldas a la máquina

Did you reserve it?	¿ Lo había reservado ?
Valladolid! All change!	¡ Valladolid! ¡Transborden !
I have left my coat in the compartment	Me he dejado olvidado el abrigo en el departamento
Where is the Lost Property Office?	¿ Dónde está la oficina de reclamaciones ?
Where can I get a cup of coffee?	¿ Dónde puedo tomar una taza de café ?
The canteen is over there	La cantina está allí enfrente
Is there a restaurant car on the express?	¿ Lleva coche-restaurante el rápido ?
Only sleeping-cars	Sólo coche-camas
Arrival and departure times of the trains are in the railway-guide	Las horas de salida y llegada de trenes están en la guía de ferrocarriles
Here is the summer time-table	Aquí tiene el horario de verano
I bought my ticket at a travel agency	Saqué el billete en una agencia de viajes
Take your seats, please	¡ Señores viajeros, al tren !
Your suit-case is too large for this luggage-rack	Su maleta no cabe en la rejilla
The big trunk goes in the luggage van	El baúl grande va en el furgón de equipajes
Windows may be opened only with the permission of all fellow passengers	Para abrir las ventanillas hay que tener permiso de los demás viajeros
Do not lean out of the window	Es peligroso asomarse al exterior
Where is the communication cord?	¿ Dónde está la señal de alarma ?
How long do we stop here?	¿ Cuánto tiempo pararemos aquí ?
You had better ask the ticket inspector when he comes to check the tickets	Mejor se lo pregunta al interventor cuando venga pidiendo los billetes

TRAVELLING BY SEA

Spaniards have always been a seafaring race, and the time of Spain's greatest political power coincided with her greatest fleet, and the *conquistadores* who founded the Spanish Empire in the New World.

Nowadays, her small merchant fleet is almost exclusively used for goods transport, but there are good passenger services between the Balearic Islands and Valencia or Barcelona, and also between the Canaries and Cádiz or Huelva.

There is no regular passenger route by sea from England to Spain, but there are a few berths in some ships sailing to Bilbao, Vigo or the Canary Islands.

TRAVELLING BY SEA	VIAJE POR MAR
Vocabulary	Vocabulario
The port, harbour	El puerto
The steamship company	La compañía naviera
The passenger-boat	El barco de pasajeros
The liner	El transátlantico
The luxury-liner	El transatlántico de lujo
The one-class liner	El transatlántico de clase única
First class	Primera (clase)
Tourist class	Clase turista
The passage, crossing	La travesía
The hull	El casco
The bow	La proa
The stern	La popa
The gangway	La pasarela
The funnel	La chimenea
The hatchways	Las escotillas
The porthole	La claraboya
The cable	La amarra
The anchor	El ancla
The fo'c'sle	El castillo de proa

The railings	El empalletado
The mast	El mástil
The engine-room	La sala de máquinas
The dining-saloon	El comedor
The smoking-room	La sala para fumadores
The cabin	El camarote
The berth	La litera
The hammock	La hamaca
The deck	La cubierta
The bridge	El puente
The wake, track of ship	La estela
The deck-chair	La silla de tijera
The life-boat	El bote de salvamento
The life-belt	El (cinturón) salvavidas
The passenger	El pasajero
The captain	El capitán
The crew	La tripulación
The sailor	El marino, marinero
The stoker	El fogonero
The steward	El camarero
The purser	El sobrecargo
The harbour pilot	El práctico
The light-house, beacon	El faro
The tug-boat	El remolcador
The seasickness	El mareo
To navigate	Navegar
To steer	Gobernar
To roll	Balancearse
To pitch	Cabecear
To book a passage	Sacar el pasaje
To embark	Embarcar
To go on board	Subir a bordo
To disembark	Desembarcar
To cast anchor	Echar el ancla

Phrases	Frases
Have you taken your steamer-ticket? Have you booked your passage?	¿ Ha sacado usted el pasaje para el vapor ?
Which route are you travelling by?	¿ Por qué ruta viaja ?
When are you sailing?	¿ Cuándo zarpa ?
I am travelling first class	Viajo en primera (clase)
This cargo boat (freighter) takes some passengers	Este barco de carga admite algún pasajero
How many knots does she do?	¿ Cuántos nudos recorre por hora ?
This steamer is not one of the fastest, but she is very comfortable	No es uno de los vapores más rápidos, pero ofrece muchas comodidades
Where does this liner call on her voyage?	¿ Dónde hace escala este transatlántico ?
I have booked an upper berth in the direct steamer to Corunna	He tomado una litera de encima en el vapor directo a La Coruña
Where is my cabin?	¿ Hacia dónde cae mi camarote ?
I cannot stand the noise of the propellers	No aguanto el ruido de las hélices
Where can I get a deck-chair?	¿ Dónde podré encontrar una silla de tijera ?
Is there a doctor on board?	¿ Hay algún médico a bordo ?
My wife has been seasick for some days	Mi esposa lleva varios días con mareo
The English Channel crossing was very stormy	La travesía del Canal de la Mancha fué muy agitada
Are you a good sailor?	¿ Es usted buen marino ?
We are having a rough passage	Estamos teniendo una travesía de perros
The ship is rolling and pitching dreadfully	El barco se balancea y cabecea de un modo horrible

The sea is very rough	La mar está muy alborotada
It is getting foggy	Está saliendo niebla
Visibility is bad	Hay poca visibilidad
A fog-horn is sounding	Están tocando una sirena
We are twenty miles off the coast	Nos encontramos a veinte millas de la costa
Where can I send a cable?	¿ Desde dónde puedo mandar un cablegrama ?
In the wireless operator's cabin	Desde la cabina del radiotelegrafista
Get your passports and landing cards ready, the coast is in sight	Tengan preparados los pasaportes y las tarjetas de desembarque ; la costa está a la vista
The harbour pilot has already come on board	El práctico ya ha subido a bordo
We shall soon be alongside	Pronto atracaremos
They are lowering the gangway	Están bajando la pasarela
The crane is unloading a car on to the dock side	La grúa está descargando un coche en el muelle

TRAVELLING BY AIR

At present (1954) you can fly under normal conditions from London to Madrid in four hours and to Barcelona in three. To Madrid there is a service on four days of the week : Mondays, Tuesdays, Fridays and Saturdays ; and to Barcelona there is a two-day service (Mondays and Saturdays). The fare is about double the train fare, but if you take into account the incidental expenses and time of the land journey, the difference is not as great as it appears at first.

Owing to its geographical position, Spain is, as it were, a kind of aircraft carrier, nosing its way westwards into the

Atlantic, and therefore its airports are used by most international airlines.

The national services link up all the airports of the Peninsula as well as Morocco, the Balearics and Canary Islands.

TRAVELLING BY AIR	EL VIAJE POR AVIÓN
Vocabulary	**Vocabulario**
The aeronautics	La aeronaútica
The air-transport	El transporte aéreo
The aircraft, plane	El avión
The seaplane	El hidro (avión)
The biplane	El biplano
The triplane	El triplano
The jet	El avión de propulsión a chorro
The airship	El dirigible
The air-trip, flight	El viaje aéreo
The air-route	La ruta aérea
The Airlines	Las Líneas aéreas
The Continental Airways	La red aérea europea
The aerodrome, airport	El aeródromo, el aeropuerto
The airfield	El campo de aviación
The stewardess	La azafata
The pilot	El piloto
The flying engineer	El mecánico
The wireless operator	El radiotelegrafista
The crew	La tripulación
The test pilot	El piloto de pruebas
The ground-staff	El equipo de tierra
The engine	El motor
The airscrew, propeller	La hélice
The cockpit	La carlinga
The wing	El ala
The flaps	Las aletas
The span	La envergadura
The fuselage	El fuselaje
The rudder (elevator lever)	El timón (de profundidad)

The tail	La cola
The fuel oil	El petróleo combustible
The wind direction	La dirección del viento
The vibration	La vibración
The safety-belt	El cinturón de seguridad
The air pocket	El bache
The air-conditioning system	El sistema de aire acondicionado
The undercarriage	El tren de aterrizaje
The tank	El depósito
The parachute	El paracaídas
The parachutist	El paracaidista
The runway	La pista de rodaje
The flight	El vuelo
The rate of climb (descent)	La velocidad de ascenso (descenso)
The forced-landing	El aterrizaje forzoso
The Civil (Military) Aviation	La Aviación Civil (Militar)
To fly	Volar
To take-off	Despegar
To land	Aterrizar
To spin	Entrar en barrena
To loop the loop	Rizar el rizo

Phrases	Frases
Which is the shortest way to the airport?	¿ Cuál es el camino más corto al aeropuerto ?
When does the next plane leave for Barcelona?	¿ A qué hora sale el primer avión para Barcelona ?
The time-table is in the waiting room	El horario está en la sala de espera
I should like to travel without breaking the journey (without intermediate landing)	Me gustaría viajar sin parada (sin aterrizajes intermedios)
How many passengers does this aircraft take?	¿ Cuántos pasajeros admite este avión ?

This plane carries fifty passengers in the cabin and a crew of five	Este avión admite cincuenta pasajeros en la cabina y una tripulación de cinco
Where will they put my luggage?	¿Dónde me pondrán el equipaje?
In the luggage hold	En la cala del equipaje
The plane is just taxi-ing out of the hangar	Están rodando ahora el aeroplano fuera del hangar
Europe is served by a network of air routes	Europa está servida por una red de rutas aéreas
A two-(three-)engined plane is just coming in	Está llegando un bi(tri)motor
The jet has not a great range	El avión de reacción a chorro no tiene un radio de acción vasto
The load-capacity of an aircraft is limited to a certain weight	La capacidad de carga de un avión está limitada a un peso determinado
Each passenger is allowed to carry twenty kilos of luggage free	A cada pasajero se le permiten veinte kilos de equipaje libres de pago
You have to pay on excess luggage	Tiene usted que pagar por exceso de equipaje
Are you liable to be airsick?	¿Le dan mareos de altura?
The stewardess is serving a meal	La azafata está sirviendo la comida
The meteorological station has announced storm warning	El Instituto Meteorológico ha anunciado que amenaza tormenta
The take-off has been delayed	El despegue ha sido diferido
We landed at Barajas (airport of Madrid) at the scheduled time	Aterrizamos en el aeropuerto de Barajas de Madrid a la hora señalada

TRAVELLING BY BICYCLE

Spaniards are keener on cycling than they were. Every year there is the big race, *la vuelta ciclista a España*, which, like the Tour de France, attracts international champions and which, for almost a month, supplies enough news to fill the sports columns of all the newspapers. Next in importance comes the National Road Race (*Campeonato Nacional*), followed by the big Catalan Race (*Vuelta a Cataluña*).

Throughout the year there are local competitions in most Spanish towns, and it can be stated that, in general, Spanish riders, trained as they are on the hilly roads of Spain, are good " climbers ".

Time races and " chases " are only seen on race tracks (*velódromos*).

As a means of transport the bicycle is used much more in the North, where the distances between places are short, than in the South or on the Central Plateau, where these distances are so great. It is a common sight to see workmen riding in groups to work or clusters of riders out for a Sunday spin.

In Spain (as in France) a licence is needed for the use of a bicycle. For an annual payment to the local council (*Ayuntamiento*) the cyclist receives a number, which he has to show in a prominent position on his bicycle.

TRAVELLING BY BICYCLE	EL VIAJE EN BICICLETA
Vocabulary	Vocabulario
The roadster	La bicicleta de paseo
The sports bicycle	La bicicleta de carreras
The tandem	El tandem
The (straight, dropped) handlebars	El guía (de paseo, de carrera)
The saddle	El sillín
The pedal	El pedal
The free-wheel	La rueda libre

The chain-wheel	El piñón
The chain	La cadena
The tyres	Las cubiertas
The inner tubes	Los neumáticos
The rims	Las llantas
The frame	El cuadro
The cross-bar	La barra
The ball-bearings	Los cojinetes de bolas
The gear-change	El cambio de velocidades
The fork	La horquilla
The hub	El cubo
The front (rear) lamp	El farol delantero (trasero)
The pump	La bomba
The back-pedalling brake	El freno de pedal
The bell	El timbre
The spokes	Los radios
The tool-bag	El carterín (de herramientas)
The spanner	La llave
The solution	La disolución
The patch	El parche
The puncture	El pinchazo
The pot-holes	Los baches
The carrier	El portabultos
The cyclist	El ciclista
To cycle	Ir en bicicleta
To ride a bicycle	Montar en bicicleta
To pedal	Pedalear
To sprint	Correr al sprint

Phrases	Frases
I like cycling	Me gusta el ciclismo
These works manufacture ladies' and men's bicycles	Esta fábrica produce bicicletas para mujeres y para hombres
I am going by " bike " to the next village	Voy en " bici " al pueblo próximo
Is your brake in working order?	¿ Funciona bien su freno ?

Yes, but the chain is a bit loose	Sí, pero la cadena está un poco floja
You were riding on the pavement, you will have to pay a fine	Iba usted por la acera ; tendrá que pagar una multa
I shall have to push my bicycle up the hill	Tendré que subir la cuesta empujando la bicicleta
I must pump the tyres up	Tengo que hinchar los neumáticos
I have a puncture in my back tyre and shall have to mend it	La cubierta de atrás se ha pinchado y tendré que pegarle un parche
The front wheel is out of centre	La rueda delantera está descentrada
I have to renew my licence at the Town Hall for another year	Tengo que renovar la matrícula de este año en el Ayuntamiento
I prefer the straight handlebar to the dropped one	Me gusta más el guía de paseo que el de carrera
The brake blocks are worn	Las zapatas del freno están gastadas
No cycling	Prohibido andar en bicicleta
You can cycle on the by-path	Puede usted ir en bicicleta por el sendero lateral
The road to the farm is full of pot-holes	El camino a la granja está lleno de baches
Put your bicycle into the shed	Meta su bicicleta en el cobertizo
You have to unfasten the bag from the carrier	Tiene usted que desatar la bolsa que lleva en el portabultos

THE TOWN

Although country people in Spain, as elsewhere, live in separate houses and farms, the town-dwellers usually occupy flats (*pisos*).

So a house in a Spanish street usually contains several fami‑ lies, each with its own flat. These houses are numbered with even numbers on the right as you walk along the street away from the town centre, and with odd numbers on your left.

The doors of the houses and, often, hotels are closed at ten or eleven o'clock at night; and, even if you have a key, it is the custom to clap your hands to call the *sereno* (or the night‑ watchman of the district), who arrives with jingling keys to let you in and accept a small tip.

As in France, the café proprietors put chairs and tables on the pavements when the weather is warm and fine. When it is hot, these are placed either in the shade of trees or under coloured awnings. The Municipal authorities often send men with water hoses to sprinkle the streets and pavements to keep down the dust and the temperature.

In the parks it is strictly forbidden to walk on the grass.

In Madrid, transport by bus, tram or underground, is rela‑ tively cheap; but at peak hours these are usually crowded even worse than in London—especially the " *Metro* " (the Madrid Underground). As in Paris, the different lines are known by the name of each terminus station, so that to find your way you must know the terminus of the line on which your destina‑ tion is situated. Instead of looking for platform 2 you look for a sign, saying *Dirección Diego de León*, or *Sol*, etc. If you have to change, you follow a sign saying *Correspondencia* and then *Dirección Sol*, etc. But in Madrid there are fewer lines than in London or Paris, and it is easy to find your way if you follow the above instructions.

The other Transport services, buses, trams and trolley‑buses are very much as in England, except that sometimes in a tram you have to pay your fare at a kind of turnstile as you enter.

THE TOWN	LA CIUDAD
Vocabulary	Vocabulario
The capital	La capital
The provincial town	La ciudad de provincia
The village	El pueblo

The suburb	El suburbio, el barrio
The outskirts	Los barrios del extrarradio
The surroundings	Los alrededores
The slums	Los barrios bajos
The market-square	La plaza del mercado
The main square	La plaza mayor
The street	La calle
The avenue	La avenida
The lane	La calleja
The blind-alley	El callejón sin salida
The side street	La bocacalle
The street corner	La esquina
The crossing	El cruce (para peatones)
The roadway, road	La calzada, la carretera
The pavement, side walk	La acera
The kerb	El borde de la acera
The gardens	Los jardines
The park	El parque
The bridge	El puente
The river	El río
The railway station	La estación de ferrocarril
The hospital	El hospital
The town hall	El ayuntamiento
The cemetery	El cementerio
The post office	La Casa de Correos
The police-station	La comisaría
The public library	La biblioteca pública
The school, private school	La escuela
The college	El Instituto
The convent school	El colegio
The church	La iglesia
The cathedral	La catedral
The university	La universidad
The museum	El museo
The exhibition	La exposición
The fire station	El parque de bomberos
The block of houses	La manzana (de casas)

The block of flats	La casa de vecindad
The public-house	La taberna
The restaurant	El restaurante
The café	El café
The flat, apartment	El piso, el apartamento
The shop-window	El escaparate
The policeman	El guardia (urbano, municipal)
The traffic policeman	El guardia del tráfico
The night-watchman	El sereno
The pedestrian	El peatón
The street cleaner	El barrendero municipal
The bus	El autobús
The tramcar	El tranvía
The Underground	El Metro(politano)
The lorry, van	El camión
The car	El coche, el automóvil
The taxi	El taxi
The stopping place	La parada
The terminus	El fin de trayecto
The entrance, way in	La entrada
The exit, way out	La salida
To get in (a car, a train)	subirse a, tomar
To get off	bajarse de, apearse
To take a walk	dar un paseo
To walk	andar, ir a pie
To ride in (a vehicle)	ir en (un vehículo)
On foot	a pie, andando
Standing	de pie

Phrases	Frases
How far is it to the High Street?	¿ Qué distancia hay de aquí a la calle principal ?
Which is the shortest way to the cathedral?	¿ Cuál es el camino más corto a la catedral ?
Can you tell me the way to the theatre?	¿ Podría indicarme el camino para ir al teatro ?

Where is the post office?	¿ Dónde está la Casa de Correos ?
The second turning on the right	La segunda calle a la derecha
Don't cross the street unless the green light is on	No cruce hasta que esté encendida la luz verde
There are the traffic lights	Ahí están las señales del tráfico
Don't step off the pavement	No se salga de la acera
The traffic is very heavy	El tráfico es muy intenso
Mind the lorry !	¡ Cuidado con el camión !
There is a traffic jam at the corner of the Gran Vía	Hay una aglomeración de tráfico en la esquina de la Gran Vía
The streets are narrow	Las calles son estrechas
I have lost my way	Me he extraviado
Turn to the left	Tuerza a la izquierda
Straight on	Todo seguido
Where is the main entrance to the hospital?	¿ Dónde cae la entrada principal al hospital ?
Where does Mr. García live?	¿ Dónde vive el señor García ?
On the top floor of this building	En el ático de este edificio
They have a flat on the ground floor	Tienen un piso (American Spanish : apartamento) en la planta baja
Can I get to the Palace Square by Underground?	¿ Puedo ir por Metro a la Plaza del Palacio ?
Take the lift. Or do you prefer the stairs?	Suba en ascensor. ¿ O prefiere subir por la escalera ?
You have to get a ticket	Tiene usted que sacar billete
Take your tickets from the machines	Saquen los billetes en las máquinas automáticas
You can also take the bus	También puede ir en autobús
The buses are crowded	Los autobuses van llenos
Let the passengers off first, please	Antes de entrar dejen salir
We are full up. Take the next bus, please	Completo. Haga el favor de tomar el próximo autobús

Not all buses are double-deckers	No todos los autobuses son de dos pisos
No room on top, pass down inside	No hay sitio arriba, pasen adentro
Don't push	No empujen
Is there no queue?	¿ No hay cola ?
Keep a passage clear	Dejen libre el paso
Fares, please	Billetes
I have lost my ticket	He perdido el billete
Don't alight when the vehicle is in motion	Prohibido apearse cuando el vehículo esté en marcha
When does the last Underground train leave?	¿ A qué hora pasa el último Metro ?
Sunday traffic is limited	El domingo la circulación está restringida
Where do I have to get off?	¿ Dónde tengo que apearme ?
No thoroughfare for vehicles	Prohibido el paso a los vehículos
Closed to pedestrians	Prohibido el paso a los peatones
No admittance (private)	Prohibido el acceso al público
Have you seen the illuminated advertisements in the centre of the city?	¿ Ha visto usted los anuncios luminosos del centro de la ciudad ?
They are putting the hose on to wash the roadways	Están poniendo la manga para regar la calle
I am going to clap my hands to see whether the night-watchman comes along	Voy a dar unas palmadas a ver si viene el sereno. ¡ Sereno !

THE HOTELS

Large hotels in Spain, which frequently have foreign names, are run on similar lines to those in any other European country. But, thanks to the numerous servants, the guests receive better service : for instance, meals are not served at such restricted hours as in English hotels.

For a much lower price, almost the same comforts as in an hotel can be enjoyed in regular boarding-houses. Besides, these often offer the guest just bed and breakfast, so that when on holiday he is not obliged to return for meals and has greater freedom of movement. But where " full pension " (*pensión completa*) terms are arranged, it is usually possible to obtain a packed lunch (*merienda*) from the kitchen.

It should be borne in mind that most Spanish towns have a fair (*feria*). When this is on, it is extremely difficult to find a room unless you have booked it in advance. Likewise in seaside resorts, where, although, as in England, many private families receive paying guests, it is not easy to find lodgings in July and August.

THE HOTELS	LOS HOTELES
Vocabulary	Vocabulario
The inn	La posada
The guest-house	La fonda, la casa de huéspedes
The boarding-house	La pensión
The hostel	La residencia
The single room	La habitación individual
The double room	La habitación para dos
The private bathroom	El cuarto de baño particular
The reception desk	La oficina de recepción
The key	La llave
The lounge	El salón
The dining-room	El comedor
The writing-room	La sala de escribir
The grill-room	La parrilla
The lobby	El vestíbulo
The gentlemen's cloakroom	El tocador de caballeros
The ladies' cloakroom	El tocador de señoras
The corridors	Los pasillos
The revolving door	La puerta giratoria
The service stairs	Las escaleras de servicio
The bell	El timbre

The bell-boy (page)	El botones
The chambermaid	La doncella
The boots	El mozo de piso
The waitress	La camarera
The waiter	El camarero
The head-waiter	El maître d'hôtel
The hall porter	El portero
The manager	El gerente
The proprietor	El propietario, el dueño
The cook	El cocinero, la cocinera
To reserve accommodation	Reservar habitación
To lodge	Alojarse
To stay at	Hospedarse en
To book in (out)	Avisar la llegada (la salida)
To settle the bill	Pagar la cuenta

Phrases	Frases
At which hotel are you staying?	¿En qué hotel se hospeda usted?
The service is good (bad)	El servicio es bueno (malo)
Can I have a single room overlooking the park?	¿Podría tomar una habitación individual con vistas al parque?
Is there central-heating and running hot and cold water in the rooms?	¿Hay calefacción central y agua corriente caliente y fría en las habitaciones?
Here is the key to your room	Aquí tiene la llave de su habitación
The lift boy will take your luggage up	El mozo del ascensor le subirá el equipaje
Can I have breakfast in my room?	¿Puedo tomar el desayuno en mi cuarto?
Where is the bathroom, please?	El cuarto de baño, ¿me hace el favor?
Please give me another towel and some soap	Hágame el favor de otra toalla y jabón

I have ordered a room with bath	He reservado habitación con baño
Please enter your name and address in the visitors' book	Tenga la bondad de inscribir su nombre y su dirección en el libro de huéspedes
How long do you intend to stay?	¿ Cuánto tiempo piensa usted quedarse ?
What are your inclusive terms?	¿ Cuáles son sus condiciones, todo incluído ?
How much is bed and breakfast?	¿ Cuánto es por la cama y el desayuno ?
I should like another blanket, or an eiderdown	Necesito otra manta o un edredón
Have you reserved a room for me?	¿ Ha reservado una habitación a mi nombre ?
Where is the bar?	¿ Dónde está el bar ?
I want to lodge a complaint with the manager	Quiero quejarme al gerente
Any letters for me?	¿ Hay alguna carta para mí ?
Can you call me to-morrow at six o'clock?	¿ Tendrían la bondad de despertarme mañana a las seis ?
Ring twice for the chambermaid	Si necesita la doncella, llame dos veces al timbre
Where did you put my comb and brush?	¿ Dónde ha puesto usted mi peine y mi cepillo ?
When can you let me have my laundry back?	¿ Cuándo me traerán la ropa limpia ?
Here is my laundry list :	Tenga la lista de la lavandera :
Four white shirts	Cuatro camisas blancas
Three coloured shirts	Tres camisas de color
Six stiff collars	Seis cuellos duros
Five soft collars	Cinco cuellos blandos
Two vests	Dos camisetas
Two pairs of underpants	Dos pares de calzoncillos
One pair of pyjamas	Un pijama
Ten handkerchiefs	Diez pañuelos
Five pairs of socks	Cinco pares de calcetines

Three slips	Tres combinaciones
Two blouses	Dos blusas
Two nightgowns	Dos camisones
Three pairs of stockings	Tres pares de medias
One linen dress	Un vestido de hilo
One dressing-gown	Un salto de cama
Is there a barber's shop in the hotel?	¿ Hay salón de peluquería en el hotel ?
I have forgotten my safety razor	He dejado olvidada la maquinilla de afeitar
Can I have this suit pressed?	¿ Podrían plancharme este traje ?
Let me have the bill, please	La cuenta, por favor
Do you prefer a boarding-house to an hotel?	¿ Prefiere usted una pensión a un hotel ?
I stayed at a hostel for a week	Me hospedé en una residencia por una semana
In this village there is only one inn	En este pueblo hay sólo una posada
This is a cheap guest-house	Esta es una casa de huéspedes barata
I am looking for an hotel which is not too expensive	Estoy buscando un hotel que no sea muy caro
Do you like your boarding-house?	¿ Está contento en su pensión ?
The food is good and plentiful	La comida es buena y abundante
The cooking is excellent	La cocina es estupenda
Can I book rooms for August?	¿ Podría reservarme habitaciones para (el mes de) Agosto ?
Sorry, we are booked up till October	Lo siento ; no hay nada libre hasta (el mes de) Octubre
You should have booked long in advance	Debía haber reservado habitación muy por adelantado

RESTAURANTS AND MEALS

Like all Mediterranean people, the Spaniards consider eating not as a mere physical necessity but rather as a source or giver of pleasure.

Breakfast consists only of a small cup of coffee or chocolate with a roll, a piece of toast or a *bollo* (a kind of bun).

From breakfast-time till the midday meal nothing is taken. But between one and two o'clock comes the main meal.[1] Shops and offices usually close from one till three o'clock and, in summer, this time is used for taking a nap as well as food.

Some people have tea or a snack at five to six o'clock; others eat nothing till supper. This meal is about ten o'clock: between the evening and night performances, which begin at seven and half-past ten or eleven respectively (see chapters on theatre and cinema).

Food varies from place to place. In the South the people require and eat less than those in the North. The Basques are especially noted for the amount of food they eat. (In Bilbao there is a club known as the Fat Man's Club—*el Club de los Hombres Gordos*—whose president weighs 28 stones.)

The staple diet of the ordinary people is formed from the leguminous vegetables of the district, e.g., *garbanzos*, a kind of chick-pea, *lentejas*, lentils, and *alubias*, something like French beans. Among the many regional dishes is the *paella valenciana*, which is made of rice seasoned with saffron and containing chicken (*pollo*) and lobster (*langosta*).

Although there is naturally a difference between home-cooked meals and those taken in a restaurant, all are usually cooked in oil and often seasoned with *ajo* (garlic). These dishes are wont to be too rich for English tastes, but those who manage to overcome this first impression are not slow in discovering how excellent and varied the dishes are.

[1] These times vary from place to place. In Madrid the ordinary hotels begin serving lunch at 2 p.m.

Special mention should be made of Spanish shellfish and fish, coming from two sources of supply, the Mediterranean and the Atlantic.

RESTAURANTS AND MEALS	RESTAURANTES Y COMIDAS
Vocabulary	**Vocabulario**
The restaurant	El restaurante
The bar	El bar
The café	El café
The breakfast	El desayuno
The aperitive	El aperitivo
The lunch	La comida (del mediodía), el almuerzo
The dinner	La comida
The supper	La cena
The plate	El plato
The dish	La fuente
The knife	El cuchillo
The fork	El tenedor
The table-spoon	La cuchara
The tea-spoon	La cucharilla
The cup	La taza
The saucer	El platillo
The glass	El vaso
The tea-pot	La tetera
The coffee-pot	La cafetera
The milk-jug	El jarro para la leche
The sugar-basin	El azucarero
The water-jug	La jarra del agua
The tray	La bandeja
The bill of fare, menu	La carta, el menú
The wine-list	La lista de vinos
The course	El plato
The cold dish	El plato frío
The vegetarian dish	El plato vegetariano
The meat dish	El plato de carne

The hors d'œuvre	Los entremeses
The dessert	El postre
The sandwich	El bocadillo
The high-tea or picnic lunch	La merienda
The salt	La sal
The pepper	La pimienta
The mustard	La mostaza
The table napkin	La servilleta
The vinegar	El vinagre
The oil	El aceite
The butter	La mantequilla
The lard	La manteca de cerdo
The fat	La grasa
The (white, brown) bread	El pan (blanco, moreno)
The roll	El panecillo
The toast	La tostada
The cold meat	Los fiambres
The ham	El jamón
The sausage	La salchicha
The bacon	El tocino
Two eggs	Un par de huevos
The fried egg	El huevo frito
The scrambled eggs	Los huevos revueltos
The poached (boiled) egg	El huevo escalfado (cocido)
The omelette	La tortilla francesa
The Spanish omelette	La tortilla española
The (thick) soup	La sopa
The clear soup	El consommé, el caldo
The entrée	El principio
The joint	El asado
The veal	La (carne de) ternera
The beef	La (carne de) vaca
The mutton	La (carne de) carnero
The lamb	La (carne de) cordero
The pork	La (carne de) cerdo
The fish	El pescado
The vegetables	Las verduras, las legumbres

The potatoes	Las patatas
The chips	Las patatas fritas
The potato crisps	Las patatas fritas a la inglesa
The sauce	La salsa
The salad	La ensalada
The lettuce	La lechuga
The sweet	El dulce
The ice-creams	Los helados
The fruit	La fruta
The stewed fruit	La fruta en compota
The cheese	El queso
The beverage, the drink	La bebida
The beer	La cerveza
The cider	La sidra
The wine	El vino
The brandy	El coñac
The liqueur	El licor
The mineral-water	El agua mineral, el agua de mesa
The lemonade, lemon squash	La limonada
The orangeade, orange squash	La naranjada
The coffee	El café
The tea	El té
The cocoa, drinking chocolate	El chocolate (hecho)
The milk	La leche
The cream	La nata
The pastry, pastries	Los pasteles
The cake	La tarta, el pastel
The biscuits	Las galletas
The jam	La mermelada
The marmalade	La mermelada de naranja
The bill, the check	La cuenta
The tip	La propina
To eat	Comer
To drink	Beber
To have breakfast (lunch, supper, high-tea, a picnic)	Desayunar (almorzar, cenar, merendar)

To be hungry	Tener hambre
To be thirsty	Tener sed
To order a course, a meal	Encargar un plato, una comida

Phrases	Frases
Have you booked a table in advance?	¿ Ha reservado mesa por adelantado ?
Waiter, a table for four, please	Camarero, mesa para cuatro, por favor
Here is the menu	Aquí está el menú
What do you choose?	¿ Qué elige usted ?
There are many courses to choose from	Hay muchos platos para elegir
Hors d'œuvres :	Entremeses :
Lobster Mayonnaise	Langosta con mayonesa
or	o
Soused sardines	Sardinas en escabeche
or	o
Grilled prawns	Gambas a la plancha
Tomato soup	Sopa de tomate
or	o
Clear soup with noodles	Caldo (Consommé) con fideos
Fish :	Pescados :
Salmon with parsley sauce	Salmón con salsa de perejil
or	o
Fried or steamed Sole	Lenguado frito o hervido
or	o
Hake with green sauce	Merluza en salsa verde
Meat :	Carnes :
Meat balls with Brussels sprouts	Albondiguillas con coles de Bruselas
or	o
Roast Lamb with baked potatoes	Cordero con patatas asadas
or	o
Larded sirloin with artichokes	Solomillo mechado con alcachofas

Dessert :
  Baked apples
  Chocolate pudding
Ices :
  Strawberry Ice with Peach Melba
Cheese :
  Dutch cheese
Does the menu appeal to you, or do you prefer to eat à la carte ?

I can recommend our fish : cod, turbot, pike, sole, carp and trout

Baked sea bream is our special dish to-day (plat du jour)
Do you prefer salt-water fish to fresh-water fish ?
What have you in the way of roast meat ?
Anything you like : pork, beef, lamb and veal
For poultry we have : turkey, goose, chicken and young duck
There is a great variety of vegetables : spinach, cabbage, carrots, cauliflower, in fact everything that is in season
Asparagus is over

I would like a salad of lettuce and tomatoes dressed with oil and vinegar

Postres :
  Manzanas asadas
  Tarta de chocolate
Helados :
  Helado de fresa con melocotones Melba
Queso :
  Queso de bola
¿ Le gusta el menú o prefiere comer a la carta ?

Les recomiendo nuestros pescados : bacalao, rodaballo, sollo, lenguado, carpa y trucha

Besugo al horno es el plato especial del día
¿ Prefiere usted el pescado de mar al de río ?
¿ Qué clase de carne asada tienen ?
Lo que desee : cerdo, vaca, cordero y ternera
De aves tenemos pavo, ganso, pollo y pato tierno
Hay una gran variedad de legumbres : espinacas, repollo, zanahorias, coliflor : en suma, todas las verduras de la época
Los espárragos se han terminado
Quisiera una ensalada de lechuga y tomates, aderezada con aceite y vinagre

What can I order for you?	¿ Qué quiere que encargue para usted ?
I should like a lamb-cutlet with peas and rice	Desearía una chuleta de cordero con guisantes y arroz
Could I have some kidneys (or liver) with onions and mashed potatoes?	¿ Podría tomar riñones (o hígado) con cebolla y puré de patatas ?
What alternative is there on the menu?	¿ Qué otra cosa ofrecen en el menú ?
A meat-and-vegetable stew	Un estofado de carne y verduras
Would you like beans or peas? You could also have lentils	¿ Quiere alubias o guisantes ? Puede tomar lentejas también
What would you like to follow?	¿ Qué desea usted para detrás ?
Are there any sweets?	¿ Hay algo de dulce ?
You can have fruit salad with whipped cream	Puede usted tomar ensalada de fruta con nata
There are no more cherries	Ya no quedan cerezas
What would you like to drink?	¿ Qué bebida le gustaría ?
A glass of stout	Un vaso de cerveza negra
A glass of light ale	Un vaso de cerveza
I can recommend Valdepeñas claret and Rioja	Les recomiendo el clarete de Valdepeñas y el Rioja
How do you like this Málaga?	¿ Qué le parece este Málaga ?
The Montilla wine is not to be iced	El vino de Montilla no se enfría
The wine is too dry for me	El vino es demasiado seco para mi gusto
I prefer sweet wines (sherry, port, muscatel, etc.)	Prefiero los vinos dulces (Jerez, Oporto, Moscatel, etc.)
Another glass of brandy?	¿ Otra copa de coñac ?
Do you want white coffee with sugar?	¿ Quiere usted café con leche y azúcar ?
I like black coffee best	Me gusta más el café puro
Have a cigarette?	¿ Un cigarillo ?
May I smoke my pipe?	¿ Me permite fumar en pipa ?

Where have I put my matches?	¿ Dónde he puesto las cerillas ?
Here is a lighter	Aquí tiene el encendedor
Pass the ashtray, please	Alcánceme el cenicero, por favor
Let me have the check, please	La cuenta, por favor
Pay at the desk, please	Haga el favor de pagar en caja
Would you like to have a drink at the counter?	¿ Quiere tomar una copa en la barra ?
I would like to sit at a table on the terrace (outside)	Me gustaría estar sentado(a) en una mesa de la terraza
Would you rather have toast or a cake?	¿ Prefiere tostadas o un pastel ?
Come and have a light supper with us	Venga a cenar con nosotros algo ligero
You'll have to take pot-luck	Tendrá que conformarse con lo que haya
Heavy meals do not agree with me	Las comidas pesadas no me sientan bien
You can have sandwiches, olives and salted almonds	Puede tomar bocadillos, aceitunas y almendras saladas
Help yourself	Sírvase usted mismo(a)
What would you like for breakfast?	¿ Qué va a tomar de desayuno ?
Coffee with " churros " (a kind of pastry made of flour and fried in hot oil)	Café con churros
Can I have a boiled egg, roll and butter and marmalade?	¿ Podría tomar un huevo pasado por agua, panecillo con mantequilla y mermelada de naranja ?
A cold (hot) meal	Una comida fría (caliente)
A cold (hot) drink	Algo frío (caliente) de beber
The meat dish was seasoned with hot paprika	La carne estaba condimentada con pimentón picante
I have no appetite	No tengo apetito
Here's luck !	¡ A su salud !

Cheers !	¡ Salud y pesetas !
He has a hearty appetite	Es un glotón
No gratuities	No se admiten propinas
Would you like to share our meal?	¡ Tome algo con nosotros !
No, thank you, I have had my dinner. Do enjoy your meal !	No, gracias, ya he comido. ¡ Qué aproveche !

SHOPPING

On the whole, shopping in Spain is not very different from shopping in England ; but it will be useful to remember, for instance, that in the tobacconist's kiosk you can buy postcards and stamps as well as tobacco, but not chocolate. The baker sells only bread. The confectioner's, where generally you will find a room reserved for customers who wish to eat pastries and drink some beverage or liqueur, sells not only pastry but also sweets and chocolates as well. Fruiterers sell only fruit. Vegetables must be bought at a stall in the market or from barrow-boys. In the *farmacia* you can obtain medicines only ; for cosmetics and perfumes you should go to the *droguería*.

Service is usually prompt and courteous, because the shop-keeper has to struggle with the Spanish housewife, who will not be cheated and who hates to be given *gato por liebre* (literally, a cat for a hare).

Politeness depends on intonation as well as words, but, when talking to shop assistants, it is better to use the conditional of verbs (*¿ Podría . . .?* or *¿ Tendría . . .?*) for a request rather than the imperative. " Give me ", or *Deme*, without using the words *por favor* for " please ", sounds rather rude in Spanish.

SHOPPING	DE COMPRAS
Vocabulary	Vocabulario
The shop	La tienda, el comercio
The stores	Los almacenes
The baker's (shop)	La panadería
The pastry-cook's	La pastelería
The confectioner's	La confitería
The butcher's	La carnicería
The fishmonger's	La pescadería
The grocer's	La tienda de ultramarinos
The fruiterer's	La frutería
The stationer's	La papelería
The men's outfitter's	La sastrería, la camisería
The haberdasher's	La mercería
The hardware dealer's	La ferretería
The cleaner's and dyer's	La tintorería
The tobacconist's	El estanco
The dispensing chemist's	La farmacia
The drug store	La droguería
The bookseller's	La librería
The shop assistant	El dependiente
The customer	El cliente, la cliente, el parroquiano, la parroquiana
To buy	Comprar
To sell	Vender
To choose, select	Escoger, seleccionar, elegir
To order	Encargar, adquirir
To cancel	Anular, cancelar
To exchange	Cambiar
To deliver	Entregar
To fetch	Recoger
To wrap up	Envolver
To bargain	Regatear

Phrases	Frases
At the baker's :	En la panadería :
What can I get for you ?	¿ Qué desea ?
Are you being served ?	¿ Le atienden ya ?

A new white loaf and half a loaf of brown bread (rye bread), please

Un pan blanco reciente y medio pan moreno (pan de centeno)

Six rolls and four crescents, please

Seis panecillos y cuatro medias lunas

At the fruiterer's :

En la frutería :

Have you any apples, please?

¿ Tiene manzanas ?

I should like three pounds of pears, please

Hágame el favor de kilo y medio de peras

Could you send me some tangerines, lemons, bananas and a pound of grapes?

¿ Podría mandarme a casa mandarinas, limones, plátanos y medio kilo de uvas ?

The walnuts are too dear, I will take chestnuts and hazelnuts instead

Las nueces son muy caras ; llevaré castañas y avellanas

Strawberries are out of season, Madam/Sir

No es la época de las fresas, señora/señor

Have you any figs or red plums?

¿ Tiene usted higos o ciruelas coloradas ?

Will you be having any cherries in to-morrow?

¿ Tendrá mañana cerezas ?

Shall I keep some for you, Madam/Sir?

¿ Quiere que se las guarde, señora/señor ?

At the grocer's :

En la tienda de ultramarinos :

I want a packet of raisins, a pound of almonds and half a pound of turrón (a kind of sweetmeat made of almonds)

Quiero un paquete de pasas, medio kilo de almendras y un cuarto de kilo de turrón

Half a pound of ground coffee and a quarter of a pound of tea, please

Cuarto de kilo de café molido y cien gramos de té

Will you have granulated or lump sugar?

¿ Quiere el azúcar molido o en terrones ?

Half a pint of vinegar, please	Medio litro de vinagre
I want a litre of olive oil and three pounds of flour	Deme un litro de aceite de oliva y kilo y medio de harina, por favor
Have you any tinned fruit?	¿ Tienen fruta en conserva ?

At the market :

En el mercado :

I want five pounds of potatoes, please	¿ Me despacha dos kilos y medio de patatas ?
The tomatoes and radishes are cheap and quite fresh	Los tomates y los rábanos son baratos y muy frescos
Could you please weigh this chicken for me?	¿ Quiere pesarme este pollo ?
Have you a small cabbage or lettuce and carrots?	¿ Tiene un repollo pequeño o una lechuga y zanahorias ?

At the stores :

En los almacenes :

There is a sale on at the stores	Hay un saldo ahora en los almacenes
What sort of woollen material have you in stock?	¿ Qué clase de tejidos de lana tienen ?
Can you show me your latest designs in silks?	¿ Pueden enseñarme los dibujos de última moda en sedas ?
We have a large selection	Tenemos un gran surtido
Four metres of red velvet, please	Cuatro metros de terciopelo rojo
That will do	Con eso me arreglo
A reel of black cotton	Un carrete de algodón negro
Three metres of that white elastic	Tres metros de aquella cinta de goma blanca
I also want a zip-fastener	Necesito también una cremallera
Do you stock small workboxes, with scissors, a thimble, darning material, tape and buttons?	¿ Tienen cajitas de costura con tijeras, dedal, material para zurcir, cinta y botones ?

I want a plain blue tie and a coloured handkerchief to match

Desearía una corbata azul liso y un pañuelo de color haciendo juego

Does this material wash well?

¿ Es lavable este material ?

It does not lose colour in the wash

Es un color que no pierde al lavar

Our delivery-van calls in your neighbourhood tomorrow

El coche repartidor pasará mañana por su barrio.

At the cleaner's:

En la tintorería:

I want these flannel trousers dry cleaned

Querría que me limpiaran estos pantalones en seco

When can I fetch them?

¿ Cuándo puedo pasar a recogerlos ?

Can this coat be dyed brown?

¿ Pueden teñir esta chaqueta en color café ?

Do you do invisible mending?

¿ Hacen zurcidos invisibles ?

At the drug store:

En la droguería:

Have you a safety-razor and some blades?

¿ Tienen maquinillas y hojas de afeitar ?

I want a shaving-brush and a stick of shaving-soap

Querría una brocha y una barra de jabón de afeitar

I want also a tube of tooth-paste and a tooth-brush

Querría también un tubo de pasta dentífrica y un cepillo para los dientes

How much will that be altogether?

¿ Cuánto es, todo junto ?

At the chemist's:

En la farmacia:

Have you anything for headaches?

¿ Tiene algo contra el dolor de cabeza ?

Can you recommend a gargle?

¿ Qué gargarismo podría recomendarme ?

A bottle of peroxide and some adhesive plaster, please

Una botella de agua oxigenada y un poco de tafetán

A box of cough lozenges

Una caja de pastillas para la tos

A big packet of cotton-wool, please

Un paquete grande de algodón hidrófilo

Please have this prescription made up for me

Hagan el favor de prepararme esta receta

I want a good tonic

Desearía un buen tónico

At the tobacconist's :

En el estanco :

Can you recommend a mild cigar?

¿ Puede recomendarme un puro suave ?

What kind of cigarettes do you stock?

¿ Qué clase de cigarrillos tiene ?

Have you any flints (wicks, petrol) for my lighter?

¿ Tiene piedras (mecha, bencina) de mechero ?

Sorry, we are sold out of everything except boxes of matches

Lo siento ; no nos queda nada de nada, a no ser cajas de cerillas

At the confectioner's :

En la confitería :

A pound box of chocolates, please

Una caja de bombones de medio kilo

How much is a pound of fruit drops and a packet of chocolate?

¿ Cuánto cuesta medio kilo de caramelos de fruta y una barra de chocolate ?

Please wrap up together the apple-tart and the half a dozen pastries

Envuélvame juntas la tarta de manzana y la media docena de pasteles

Don't touch goods displayed on the counter

Se ruega no toquen los artículos expuestos en el mostrador

Can you change a 100 pesetas note?

¿ Podría cambiarme un billete de cien pesetas ?

Can you give me change for 50 pesetas ?

¿ Tiene vuelta de un billete de cincuenta pesetas ?

THE POST OFFICE

The Post Office in Spanish cities is usually a detached building, like that of the Town Hall or the Bank of Spain. Office hours are the ordinary ones for Spanish offices, with the exception of some branches, like " Telegrams ", which are always open.

There are few pillar-boxes in the streets, but nearly all tobacconists, who sell stamps as well as tobacco, have a letter-box. These are not painted red but silver.

The postmen deliver letters every day, including one Sunday delivery, either giving the doorkeeper all the letters for the occupants of the building or whistling from the doorway (one whistle for the first floor, two for the second, etc.). In that case the man concerned has to go downstairs to collect his letters. Only one large city has been divided into postal districts, so the letters sent from inside the city itself have to have written on them : " *Plaza* " or " *Ciudad* " (" City "). The Post Office service is very efficient. Letters addressed in hieroglyphics like :

> a drawing of Christ (for *Jesús*, a common name in Spain),
> a drawing of a tower (meaning *Torres*, a surname),
> a drawing of a fish followed by a 3 (meaning No. 3 Fish Street),
> a drawing of the Alhambra (meaning Granada)

are not thrown into the waste-paper basket as jokes from people with nothing to do, but handed over to a special section, which is employed in deciphering them.

In the address the number of the house is written after the name of the street, and after that the number of the floor should be mentioned : ground floor, first, second, etc., as follows : ent^{lo}, 1°, 2°, 3°, etc.

POST OFFICE	CORREOS
Vocabulary	Vocabulario
The General Post Office	La Dirección General de Correos y Telecomunicaciones
The letter-box, pillar-box	El buzón

C

The letter	La carta
The postcard	La tarjeta postal
The printed matter	Los impresos
The registered letter	La carta certificada
The express letter	La carta con sello de urgencia
The telegram	El telegrama
The parcel-post	El paquete postal
The samples having no commercial value	Las muestras sin valor comercial
The airmail letter	La carta por avión
The envelope	El sobre
The address	La dirección, las señas
The addressee	El destinatario
The sender	El remitente
The counter	La ventanilla
The post-office official	El funcionario de Correos
The postman	El cartero
The village postman	El cartero rural
The postage	El franqueo concertado
The stamp	El sello
The wrapper	La envoltura
The Green Label	La etiqueta verde
The sealing wax	El lacre
The postal order	El giro postal
The telegraphic transfer	El giro telegráfico
The fees, charges	Los costos
Post-free	Libre de franqueo
By air mail	Correo aéreo
By sea mail	Correo marítimo
Abroad	Extranjero
Country	Provincias
Poste restante	Lista de Correos
Collection hours	Horas de recogida
From	Remite
To post	Echar al buzón
To receive a letter	Recibir una carta
To stamp a letter	Sellar una carta, poner el franqueo

Phrases	Frases
Has the postman been?	¿ Ha pasado ya el cartero ?
He delivered two letters and a postcard this morning	Entregó dos cartas y una tarjeta postal esta mañana
The postman has left this form	El cartero ha dejado este impreso
Letters are delivered three times a day	Se hacen tres repartos de cartas al día
Where can I collect this parcel?	¿ Dónde puedo recoger este paquete ?
Take this letter to the nearest pillar-box, please	Haga el favor de depositarme esta carta en el buzón más próximo
The next collection is at six	La próxima recogida es a las seis
You must pay excess-postage	Tiene usted que pagar diferencia de franqueo
Return to sender, address not known	Devuélvase al remitente, destinatario desconocido en la dirección del sobre
Please forward	Sírvanse entregarlo al destinatario
What is the postage for an airmail letter to England?	¿ Qué franqueo hay que poner en una carta por avión a Inglaterra ?
Where can I enquire for poste restante letters?	¿ Dónde puedo recoger las cartas dirigidas a la lista de correos ?
Where do I get postage stamps?	¿ Dónde puedo adquirir sellos de correos ?
They are sold at the tobacconist's in Spain, and in the post office	En España se venden en los estancos y en Correos
Two fifty cents stamps, please	Dos sellos de a cincuenta céntimos
Three postcards and a cable form, please	Tres tarjetas postales y un impreso de cablegrama, por favor

Please send me this book cash on delivery	Hagan el favor de enviarme este libro contra reembolso
Can I register this letter?	¿ Podría certificar esta carta ?
Do you want to register this parcel?	¿ Quiere usted certificar este paquete ?
You must complete the special form that has to accompany the parcel	Tiene usted que llenar el impreso especial que ha de acompañar el paquete
Please let me have an international money-order form	Tenga la bondad de facilitarme un impreso de giro internacional
You must seal a registered parcel	Los paquetes certificados tienen que ir sellados
I want to send a telegram	Querría enviar un telegrama
Don't forget to put the name and address of sender	No se olvide de poner el nombre y la dirección del remitente
In case it cannot be delivered, it will be returned	En caso de que no se encuentre al destinatario le será devuelto al remitente
A telegram with pre-paid reply	Un telegrama con respuesta pagada
What is the telegram rate to England?	¿ Qué tarifa tienen los telegramas a Inglaterra ?
Greetings Telegrams are cheaper	Los telegramas de felicitación son más baratos
This letter is dated the 12th, but the post-stamp shows it was sent off on the 14th	Esta carta está fechada el doce, pero el matasellos indica que ha sido puesta en el buzón el catorce
How long does a surface-mail letter take from here to South America's east coast?	¿ Cuánto tarda una carta por correo marítimo desde aquí hasta la costa oriental de América del Sur ?

THE TELEPHONE

The automatic telephone is general in Spain, but there are only figures (no letters) on the dial, although no Spanish telephone number has more than six figures. While dialling it is customary to divide the number into pairs. Thus 221020 is read as " twenty-two ", " ten ", " twenty ". Notice that 22 is not " double two ", and that nought is read not as o but as *cero*. Two o's would be *cero, cero*.

Instead of inserting coins in the call boxes, you put in special discs or counters which can be obtained at the exchange, the cafés, the bars and in fact wherever there is a public telephone. In many places, however, the customers are allowed free use of the telephone, because the owners do not pay according to the number of calls but have a special flat rate.

For trunk or toll calls you have to call the exchange if you are not a private subscriber.

There are no street booths : only small branch exchanges situated in different districts of the city. They can be recognised by a gilt metal plaque or disc on the door with a map of Spain in relief and with the word " *Teléfonos* " on it in big letters. Usually the main telephone exchange occupies an important building—in Madrid the *Telefónica* is a famous landmark, a skyscraper in the Gran Vía.

The telephone directory, besides giving a list of subscribers in alphabetical order on the white pages and showing professional men and businesses on the yellow pages, contains also a section of blue pages which give the telephone numbers by streets. You have only to follow an attractive brunette home and see the number of the house she enters. Ten minutes later you can find not only her telephone number but probably her social status as well. But any errors made are not the responsibility of the Telephone Company !

THE TELEPHONE	EL TELÉFONO
Vocabulary	**Vocabulario**
The public telephone	El teléfono público
The receiver	El auricular
The mouthpiece	El micrófono
The disc, token	La ficha
The exchange	La central
The automatic exchange	La central automática
The extension	La línea supletoria
The operator	El (la) telefonista
The subscriber	El abonado
The telephone booth	La cabina de teléfono
The directory	La guía
The call	La llamada
The night call	La llamada nocturna
The local call	La llamada local
The trunk call	La conferencia interurbana
The connection	La comunicación
Engaged	Comunica
To connect	Poner en comunicación
To dial	Marcar
To phone, ring up	Telefonear, llamar por teléfono
To book a call	Poner una conferencia
To cancel a call	Anular una conferencia

Phrases	**Frases**
Hello !	¡ Dígame ! , ¡ oiga !
Are you on the phone ?	¿ Tiene usted teléfono ?
Please give me a ring to-morrow evening	Deme un telefonazo mañana de noche
How do I dial ?	¿ Cómo tengo que hacer para marcar ?
Lift the receiver	Descuelgue el auricular
Then dial the number required	Después marque el número que desee
Have you a token for the telephone ?	¿ Podría proporcionarme una ficha ?

Please insert the token before dialling	Tenga la bondad de insertar la ficha antes de marcar
Could I make use of your telephone?	¿Me permite que haga una llamada desde su teléfono?
Please yourself	No faltaba más
Hello, could I speak to Mr. Martínez?	¡Oiga! ¿Podría hablar con el señor Martínez?
Speaking	Al aparato
Are you 25-12-11?	¿Es el veinticinco-doce-once?
Number engaged	Comunica
There is no answer	No contesta
Put the receiver down and repeat the call	Cuelgue y vuelva a llamar
I can't get through	No consigo comunicar
Enquiries, please	¿Información?
Can you give me the number of Mr. Alberto Vélez, No. 10 Alcalá Street?	¿Podría decirme el número de Don Alberto Vélez de la calle de Alcalá número diez?
Look it up in the blue pages of the directory	Búsquelo en las páginas azules de la guía
I tried several times to ring my hotel, but there is no reply	Varias veces he intentado llamar al hotel, pero no contesta
Sorry, wrong number	Se ha equivocado de número
The telephone is out of order	El teléfono no funciona
Is that the Travel Bureau?	¿Es la Agencia de viajes?
Just a minute, hold the line, please	Un minuto, por favor, no se retire
Where is there a public call office?	¿Dónde hay por aquí un teléfono público?
Miss, I want to book a call to Barcelona	Señorita, ¿podría ponerme una conferencia con Barcelona?
Where can I wait until my trunk call comes through?	¿Dónde puedo esperar hasta que me den la conferencia interurbana?
Barcelona, booth No. 7	Barcelona, por el siete

Sorry, we were cut off	**Lo siento, nos habían cortado la comunicación**
Could you please give a message to Mr. Moreno?	**¿ Tendría la bondad de pasarle un recado al Sr. Moreno ?**
You are wanted on the phone	**Preguntan por usted al teléfono**

CORRESPONDENCE

Spaniards are not keen on letter-writing; probably as they live in a medium which claims all their attention they do not enjoy much reclusion and are reluctant to concentrate on writing letters. This, of course, refers only to private correspondence, for business correspondence goes on as in any other country.

After the first letter the sender's address is frequently omitted at the top of the page, but should always be written on the back of the envelope preceded by the word *Remite* (from).

The date is usually written at the head of a letter, but there are some people who put it at the end. After the opening a colon is used instead of a comma.

There is no need to use flowery language in the body of the letter, but there are several formal endings which have little real significance. *Su atto. y s. s.* is the abbreviation of *su atento y seguro servidor* (Your faithful servant). *Afmo. s. s.* is the abbreviated form of *afectísimo seguro servidor* (Your most affectionate and faithful servant). *Q. e. s. m.* is a short form of *que estrecha su mano* (Who shakes your hand), while *q. b. s. m.* is an abbreviation of *que besa su mano* (Who kisses your hand), used only when the sender is a man and the receiver a woman. These endings are followed by the signature (*firma*), which is adorned with a flourish or *rúbrica*.

Notice that Spaniards have two surnames, the first one from their father's side and which is the one they are known by, the second from their mother's. Married women keep their own

name and add their husband's joined by " de ". Thus, Consuelo Guzmán de Aguilar.

On the envelope one writes, before the name, *señor* (abbreviated to *Sr.*) or *señor don* (abbreviated to *Sr.D.*) ; or else *señora* (*Sra.*) or *señora doña* (*Sra. Da.*) ; or else *señorita* (*Srta.*).

The address has the street first and the number second ; e.g., Atocha, 25. The word *calle* (street) is rarely used on the envelope.

Barcelona is probably the only town in Spain which is divided into Postal Districts as is London or Liverpool.

CORRESPONDENCE / LA CORRESPONDENCIA

Vocabulary / Vocabulario

The letter	La carta
The business letter	La carta comercial
The letter of condolence	La carta de pésame
The letter of congratulation	La carta de felicitación
The postcard	La tarjeta postal
The picture postcard	La postal
The handwriting	La letra
The pen, nib	La pluma, el plumín
The penholder	El portaplumas, el mango
The fountain-pen	La (pluma) estilográfica
The ball-pointed pen	El bolígrafo
The pencil	El lápiz
The copying-ink pencil	El lápiz de tinta
The coloured pencil	El lápiz de colores
The gum, glue	La goma de borrar
The letter-file	El fichero de cartas
The card-index	El índice de tarjetas
The paper	El papel
The notepaper	El papel de cartas, el papel de escribir
The cardboard	El cartón
The envelope	El sobre
The writing-pad	El bloc de escribir

The blotting-paper	El papel secante
The ink	La tinta
The inkstand	El tintero
The sealing wax	El lacre
The stationer's	La papelería
The writing-desk	La mesa de escritorio, el bufete
The shorthand	La taquigrafía
The typewriter	La máquina de escribir
The carbon-paper	El papel carbón
The string	El cordel
The folder	La carpeta
The sender	El remitente
The addressee	El destinatario
The address	Las señas, la dirección
The enclosures	Los anexos
The heading	El encabezamiento
The signature	La firma
The commercial term	El término comercial
The clerk	El oficinista
The typist	La mecanógrafa
The secretary	El secretario, la secretaria
The book-keeper	El contable
The partner	El socio
The owner	El propietario
The staff	El personal
E. & O. E. (Errors and Omissions Excepted)	S. E. u. O. (Salvo Error u Omisión
To write	Escribir
To type	Escribir a máquina
To copy	Copiar
To answer	Contestar
To stick	Pegar
To seal	Sellar
To fold	Doblar
To tie	Atar
To send	Enviar, mandar

Phrases	Frases
Where is the writing-room?	¿ Dónde está la sala de escritorio ?
There are envelopes and note-paper on the writing-desk	Hay sobres y papel de escribir sobre la mesa de escritorio
I have to write an urgent letter	Tengo que escribir una carta urgente
Shall I type it?	¿ He de escribirla a máquina ?
I am expecting important news	Espero noticias importantes
I have to answer some letters	Tengo que contestar algunas cartas
I owe my friend a letter	Le debo carta a mi amigo
Can you lend me your fountain-pen?	¿ Podría prestarme su estilográfica ?
My fountain-pen is broken. Where can I get it repaired?	Se me ha roto la estilográfica. ¿ Dónde podrían arreglármela ?
He writes a very clear hand	Tiene la letra muy clara
Take this letter down in shorthand	Tome esta carta en taquigrafía
He can neither read nor write. He is illiterate	No sabe leer ni escribir. Es analfabeto
Get this letter done quickly, it must catch the evening post	Despácheme la carta en seguida; tiene que coger el correo de la noche
Make two carbon copies of this invoice	Saque dos copias al carbón de esta factura
Have you filed the letters?	¿ Ha archivado usted las cartas ?
I told you all about the matter in my recent letter	Le he explicado todo el asunto en mi carta última
I read your letter with great pleasure	He leído su carta con sumo placer
My sincere congratulations	Mis sinceras felicitaciones
Many happy returns of the day	Muchas felicidades en este día

I was very pleased to receive the news of your engagement (marriage)	Con suma satisfacción acabo de recibir la noticia de su petición de mano (enlace)
My sincere condolences	Mi más sentido pésame
May I express my deep sympathy	Le acompaño en el sentimiento
In reply to your letter of the 16th June.	En contestación a su atenta (carta) del día 16 de Junio
In receipt of your favour I am pleased to inform you that . . .	Al recibo de su carta me complace informarle que . . .
I herewith acknowledge receipt of your circular	Acuso recibo de su carta circular
My dear father,	Querido padre :
Dear Robert,	Querido Roberto :
Dearest Margaret,	Queridísima Margarita :
Dear Professor (Doctor, Captain),	Estimado profesor : (doctor :, capitán :)
Dear Mr. Fernández,	Estimado señor Fernández :
Dear Mrs. Alvarez,	Estimada señora Alvarez :
Messrs. Pedro Leal & Co. Ltd., Calle de las Sierpes, 3, Sevilla	Señores Pedro Leal & Cia. Ltda., Calle de las Sierpes, 3, Sevilla
Gentlemen (Dear Sirs),	Muy señores nuestros :
Yours faithfully . . .	Suyos attos. y ss. ss. . . .
Yours sincerely . . .	Suyo afmo. . . .
I remain, Yours sincerely . . .	Quedo de Ud. su muy atto. y s.s., q.e.s.m. . . .
With respectful greetings . . .	Con mis respetuosos saludos . . .
With kind regards from . . .	Con los mejores recuerdos de . . .
With all good wishes, Yours affectionately, Robert	Con los mejores deseos de su afectuoso amigo, Roberto
Your affectionate son	Tu hijo que te quiere
Much love from Joan	Muy cariñosamente, Juana

A personal letter :

Gijón, 4th May 1953

Dear Mrs. García,

Many thanks for your kind invitation to dinner. I am sorry to say I shall be away this week-end, but I shall be very pleased to spend one evening next week with you if convenient.

With kind regards,

Yours sincerely,

Una carta personal :

Gijón, 4 de Mayo de 1953

Apreciable señora García :

Permítame que le dé las gracias por su amable invitación a cenar. Siento tener que participarle que estaré ausente este fin de semana, pero tendré sumo gusto en pasar una velada con usted la semana próxima, si no tiene inconveniente.

La saluda afectuosamente,

s.s., q.e.s.m.

A short business note :

Calle de Larios, 23
Málaga
8th June, 1953

The Manager,

Municipal Electricity Works

Dear Sir,

I beg to inform you that our electric meter is not working. Please send someone to attend to it. With thanks in anticipation,

Yours faithfully,

B. Morán

Una breve nota de negocios :

Calle de Larios, 23
Málaga
8 de Junio de 1953

Señor Director-Gerente

Fábrica Municipal de Electricidad

Muy señor mío :

Por la presente me permito informarle que mi contador eléctrico no funciona. Le agradecería enviase a alguien para que lo examinara. Con gracias anticipadas quedo suyo,

atto. s.s.

B. Morán

A business letter :

Messrs. Pons & Vilaró
    Rambla, 45
        Barcelona

Dear Sirs,

      We have pleasure in sending you herewith invoice for two hundred pairs of best-quality men's shoes bought for your account and to be shipped on the 22nd inst. The sizes you specified were in stock, and we hope you will be pleased with the goods, as the make is strong and service-able, and the manufacturers guarantee the goods to stand any climate.

    You will gather from the invoice that we have been able to obtain a special cash dis-count of five per cent, making the total amount £250, for which please send us your remittance.

    I am,

      With compliments,
        Yours faithfully,
          Merino & Sons S.A.

Addresses on envelopes :

    Guillermo Ortiz, Esq.
      Calle de Uría, 6
        Oviedo

Una carta comercial :

Señores Pons y Vilaró
    Rambla, 45
        Barcelona

Muy señores nuestros :

      Tenemos el gusto de adjuntarles factura por dos-cientos pares de zapatos de caballero de la mejor calidad, adquiridos por su cuenta y que serán embarcados el día 22 de los corrientes. Los tamaños que Vds. detallaban estaban en existencia y confiamos en que la mercancía será de su gusto, ya que su hechura es fuerte y los fabricantes garantizan que re-siste cualquier clima.

    Por la factura advertirán que hemos podido conseguir un des-cuento especial del cinco por ciento por pago al contado, ascendiendo el total a £250.—, suma que les rogamos tengan a bien remitirnos.   Siempre a sus órdenes, quedamos de ustedes, sus attos. y ss. ss.

    Merino e Hijos S.A.

Direcciones en sobres :

    Sr. D. Guillermo Ortiz
      Calle de Uría, 6
        Oviedo

<table>
<tr><td>Professor L. Albizúa
c/o C. Montenegro, Esq.
Calle Ancha, 5
Deusto (Vizcaya)
Please forward</td><td>Sr. Professor L. Albizúa
(Suplicada) Sr. C. Monte-
negro
Calle Ancha, 5
Deusto (Vizcaya)
Sírvanse entregarla</td></tr>
<tr><td>Mrs. María Blanco de Rivera
Plaza del Mercado, 3
Segovia</td><td>Sra. Da. María Blanco de Rivera
Plaza del Mercado, 3
Segovia</td></tr>
<tr><td>Miss Elena Ordóñez
Students Hostel
Goya, 341
Madrid
Spain</td><td>Srta. Elena Ordóñez
Residencia de Estudiantes
Goya, 341
Madrid
España</td></tr>
</table>

BANKING AND MONEY

The foreigner who wishes to exchange his money into pesetas can do so in any Spanish Bank, but if he wishes to change it into any other currency, he must obtain permission from the *Instituto Nacional de Moneda Extranjera* (National Institute of Foreign Currency), which controls all these exchange operations.

Apart from the *Banco de España*, which has the same status as our Bank of England, the most important banks are : the *Banco Español de Crédito*, with 447 branches and agencies, the *Banco Central*, with 352, the *Banco Hispano Americano*, with 268, the *Banco de Vizcaya*, with 162 and the *Banco de Bilbao*, with 104.

For small savings there are *Cajas de Ahorros* (Saving Banks), which have nothing to do with the Post Office.

In Spain Postal Orders do not exist. When you want to send money by post you go to the Post Office, to the counter

marked *Giros*. For a small fee the Post Office will send money to the address you give them in the same time taken by an ordinary letter (*giro postal*).

For more rapid transference there is the *giro telegráfico*, which will despatch money in an hour or two, the time taken, in fact, by a telegram.

BANKING	LA BANCA
Vocabulary	Vocabulario
The bank	El banco
The account	La cuenta
The deposit account	La cuenta depósito
The current account	La cuenta corriente
The currency	Las divisas
The (crossed) cheque	El cheque (cruzado)
The bank manager	El director de banco
The cashier	El cajero
The accountant	El contable
The bearer	El portador
The stockbroker	El agente de Bolsa
The money market	El mercado de divisas
The Stock Exchange	La Bolsa
The bill of exchange	La letra de cambio
The exchange rate	El índice de cambio
The I.O.U.	El pagaré
The share	La acción
The shareholder	El accionista
The securities	Los valores
The bonds	Las obligaciones
The simple (compound) interest	El interés simple (compuesto)
The (net) profit	El beneficio (líquido)
The loss	La pérdida
The advance deposit	El anticipo
The debtor	El deudor
The creditor	El acreedor
The letter of credit	La carta de crédito

The credit	El haber
The debit	El debe
To endorse	Endosar
To cash a cheque	Hacer efectivo un cheque
To make out (write) a cheque	Extender un cheque
To extend	Prolongar
To sign	Firmar
To overdraw	Quedar en descubierto
To open (close) an account	Abrir (cerrar) una cuenta
To pay by cheque	Pagar mediante cheque
To pay by cash	Pagar al contado
To accept a draft at 30 days	Aceptar una letra a 30 días vista
To borrow	Pedir prestado
To lend	Prestar

Phrases	Frases
Have you a banking account?	¿ Tiene usted cuenta bancaria ?
I should like to pay this into my account	Quisiera ingresar esto en mi cuenta
Can I deposit securities and valuables here?	¿ Podría depositar aquí valores y objetos de valor ?
Could you keep these documents in your Safe?	¿ Podría guardarme estos documentos en la caja fuerte ?
Can you send me my monthly statement of account?	¿ Podría enviarme el estado mensual de mi cuenta ?
What is my balance to date?	¿ Qué saldo tengo a la fecha ?
You have a slight overdraft	Ha quedado usted al descubierto por una suma pequeña
I can't grant you any credit	No puedo concederle crédito
I should like to cash this draft at maturity	Quisiera que me hicieran efectiva esta Letra a su vencimiento
Can I change my Traveller's Cheque in this Branch of the Bank of Spain?	¿ Puedo cambiar mi cheque de viajero en esta sucursal del Banco de España ?
You have forgotten to sign	Se ha olvidado usted de firmar

Please let me have some notes and small cash	Haga el favor de pagarme en billetes y algo de calderilla
Has this bill of exchange been honoured?	¿ Ha sido abonada esta Letra ?
When was this sight draft due?	¿ Cuándo vencía este giro a la vista ?
You get a discount of 2 per cent if you meet the bill prior to expiry date	Se le concederá un descuento del dos por ciento si abona la Letra antes de la fecha de su vencimiento
We only sell for cash	Sólo se vende al contado
Does the bank pay interest?	¿ Paga interés el banco ?
Only on deposit accounts, not on current accounts	Sólo en cuentas de depósito ; en cuentas corrientes, no.
Do these shares pay a high rate of interest?	¿ Pagan estas acciones un índice de interés crecido ?
We do not speculate in industrial shares	No especulamos con acciones industriales
Would you like to deposit your money in a savings-bank?	¿ Querría usted ingresar su dinero en la Caja de Ahorros ?
I prefer to invest my capital in real estate	Prefiero colocar mi capital en bienes inmuebles
Which counter is for foreign currency?	¿ Cuál es la ventanilla de moneda extranjera ?
Can I transfer this Sterling amount to a Spanish account?	¿ Puedo transferir esta suma de Libras Esterlinas a una cuenta española ?
No transfers granted	No se conceden transferencias
Is this gentleman a stock-broker?	¿ Es agente de Bolsa este señor ?
The Stock Exchange is dull to-day	La Bolsa está muerta hoy
Bonds are rising (falling)	Las obligaciones están en alza (en baja)
There was a lively turnover in the money market	Hubo mucho movimiento en el mercado de divisas

Have you any gilt-edged securities?	¿ Dispone usted de bonos del Estado ?
I have some Government loans	Tengo algunas Deudas del Estado
I must sell some shares to settle with my creditors	Tengo que vender algunas acciones para liquidar deudas con mis acreedores
The firm is bankrupt	La firma está en bancarrota
The debts exceed the assets	Las deudas exceden el activo
He is a trustworthy businessman	Es un negociante de confianza
He is a sound banker	Es un banquero solvente
He is in arrears with his payments of interests	Está atrasado en el pago de los intereses
This cheque is payable to bearer	Este cheque es pagadero al portador

I.O.U. :

Madrid, 10th January, 1952
I.O.U. 1000 pesetas to Mr.
J. Montenegro, payable not
later than 1st June, 1952.
Alberto Fernández

Pagaré :

Madrid, 10 de Enero de 1952
Pagaré a la orden del Sr. J.
Montenegro de esta ciudad,
antes del día 1 de Junio, la
cantidad de 1000 pesetas, por
valor recibido de dicho señor.
Alberto Fernández

Bill of Exchange :

Valencia, 15th August, 1952
2500 pesetas
Three months after date
pay to Messrs. Aguilar &
Co. the sum of Two Thousand Five Hundred pesetas
for value received.
(signed) Tomás González
and Sons

Letra de Cambio :

Valencia, 15 de Agosto de 1952
2500 pesetas
A tres meses fecha sírvase
pagar a la orden de los Sres.
Aguilar & Cia. la cantidad de
Dos Mil Quinientas pesetas
por valor recibido.
(firmado) Tomás González e
Hijos

Acknowledgment :

Dear Sirs,

    We acknowledge receipt of the extract of our current account which you closed on the 31st December, 1952, with which we agree. Thanking you, we are,

    Yours faithfully,

        Casares Hermanos

Acuse de recibo :

Muy señores nuestros :

    Tenemos el gusto de acusar recibo del extracto de nuestra cuenta corriente con su estimada casa, cerrado el 31 de Diciembre de 1952 y con el cual estamos conformes.

    Nos reiteramos de Vds.

    attos. y ss. ss.,

        Casares Hermanos

NUMERALS

The important differences between Spanish and English numerals are :

(1) **Telephone numbers** are read in couples : e.g., 251110 is *veinticinco* (25), *once* (11), *diez* (10).

(2) **Dates.** The years are read as a full number : e.g., *mil* (one thousand) *novecientos* (nine hundred) *cincuenta* (fifty) *y tres* (and three). Never " nineteen hundred . . ." etc. The **days of the month** are expressed as cardinal, not ordinal, numbers (except for the first day) : e.g., May 1st, *primero de Mayo* (*mayo*) ; May 2nd, *dos de Mayo* (*mayo*) ; September 28th, *veintiocho de Septiembre* (*setiembre*) ; January 10th, 1813, *diez de Enero de mil ochocientos trece*.

(3) Where **large numbers** in English have commas, the Spaniards put full-stops : e.g., 8,311,675 becomes 8.311.675.

(4) **Decimal** points, on the other hand, become commas in Spanish : e.g., 3·5 (three point five) becomes 3,5 (*tres coma cinco*).

(5) In English we join with a hyphen numbers consisting

of tens and units : e.g., thirty-two. But in Spanish they say and write, *treinta y* (and) *dos*, inserting the *y*.

(6) Yet between hundreds and units where we put " and " the Spaniards have nothing : e.g., Two hundred and nine becomes *doscientos nueve*.

(7) **Cardinal numbers,** with the exception of *uno* and *una*, have no gender : but the **ordinals** must agree in gender with the noun they qualify : e.g., The Fourth Commandment, *El Cuarto Mandamiento*; The Ninth Symphony, *La Novena Sinfonía*. Even in abbreviations the gender is shown : e.g., 4º *piso*, the Fourth Floor ; 2ª *parte*, the Second Part, and the keyboards of Spanish typewriters are furnished with these abbreviated signs.

(8) In ordinary handwriting the Spaniards put a stroke or bar across the seven : e.g., $\not{7}$ = 7, and 1 = 1.

NUMERALS	NUMERALES
Vocabulary	Vocabulario

Cardinals :	Cardinales :
nil, nought	cero
one	uno -a
two	dos
three	tres
four	cuatro
five	cinco
six	seis
seven	siete
eight	ocho
nine	nueve
ten	diez
eleven	once
twelve	doce
thirteen	trece
fourteen	catorce
fifteen	quince
sixteen	dieciséis

seventeen	diecisiete
eighteen	dieciocho
nineteen	diecinueve
twenty	veinte
twenty-one	veintiuno
twenty-two	veintidós
thirty	treinta
thirty-one	treintaiuno, treinta y uno
thirty-two	treintaidós, treinta y dos
forty	cuarenta
fifty	cincuenta
sixty	sesenta
seventy	setenta
eighty	ochenta
ninety	noventa
one hundred	cien(to)
one hundred and one	ciento uno -a
two hundred	doscientos
three hundred	trescientos
four hundred and thirty	cuatrocientos treinta
a thousand	mil
one thousand nine hundred and six	mil novecientos seis
two thousand	dos mil
a million	un millón

Ordinals :

Ordinales :

the first	el primero, la primera
the second	el segundo, la segunda
the third	el tercero, la tercera
the fourth	el cuarto, la cuarta
the fifth	el quinto, la quinta
the sixth	el sexto, la sexta
the seventh	el séptimo, la séptima
the eighth	el octavo, la octava
the ninth	el noveno, la novena
the twentieth	el vigésimo, la vigésima

the twenty-fourth	el vigésimo cuarto, la vigésima cuarta
the thirtieth	el trigésimo, la trigésima
the hundredth	el centésimo, la centésima
the thousandth	el milésimo, la milésima

Fractions :	Fracciones :
a half	una mitad, un medio
a third	un tercio
a fourth	un cuarto
a fifth	un quinto
a sixth	un sexto
a twentieth	una vigésima parte
a hundredth	una centésima parte
3·5 (three point five)	3,5 tres, coma, cinco ; tres unidades, cinco décimas (partes)
4·75 (four point seven five)	4,75 cuatro, coma, setenta y cinco ; cuatro unidades, setenta y cinco centésimas (partes)

Adverbs :	Adverbios :
once	una vez
twice	dos veces (doble)
thrice (three times)	tres veces (triple)
The figure	La cifra
The number	El número
The mathematics	Las matemáticas
The arithmetic	La aritmética
The multiplication table	La tabla de multiplicar
The addition	La suma
The subtraction	La resta, la sustracción
The multiplication	La multiplicación
The division	La división
The sum	La suma, la cantidad
The percentage	El porcentaje
To add	Sumar

To subtract	Restar
To multiply	Multiplicar
To divide	Dividir
To calculate	Calcular
To estimate	Estimar
To deduct	Deducir, sustraer

Phrases	Frases
How long have you been waiting?	¿Cuánto tiempo lleva usted esperando?
Three quarters of an hour	Tres cuartos de hora
What are your office hours?	¿Cuáles son sus horas de oficina?
From nine to five	De nueve a cinco
I had ten days leave	Tenía diez días de permiso
I spent eighteen months in Spain	He pasado dieciocho meses en España
How far is it to Barcelona?	¿Qué distancia hay de aquí a Barcelona?
(It is) twenty-six kilometres from here	Veintiséis kilómetros desde aquí
How long will it take me to get there?	¿Cuánto tiempo tardaré en llegar?
About an hour and a half	Alrededor de hora y media
The train will leave for Madrid in thirty minutes	El tren para Madrid saldrá dentro de treinta minutos
My seat is row ten number twelve	Mi localidad es fila diez número doce
This ring costs more than a hundred pesetas	Este anillo cuesta más de cien pesetas
There were hundreds of children in that school	Había cientos de niños en esa escuela
It is the last day of my holidays.	Es el último día de mis vacaciones
He inherited a fourth (a quarter) of his father's fortune	Heredó la cuarta parte de la fortuna de su padre

Two thirds of the book are uninteresting	Las dos terceras partes del libro carecen de interés
He sold half of his property	Vendió la mitad de su patrimonio
A year and a half ago I was in hospital	Hace año y medio estaba yo en el hospital
The child is six months old	La criatura tiene seis meses de edad
He stayed abroad over three years	Estuvo en el extranjero más de tres años
In nineteen hundred and fourteen	En mil novecientos catorce
The percentage of pupils studying mathematics is larger than that studying languages	El porcentaje de alumnos que estudian matemáticas es mayor que el de los que estudian idiomas

COINAGE, WEIGHTS, MEASURES

Like almost all European countries, Spain adheres to the metric system. There still remain ancient regional measures (such as " two days of oxen ", or the field which a yoke of oxen can plough in two days), but these are now disappearing.

The monetary unit is the *peseta* (110 pesetas equal 1 pound sterling on the present exchange) divided into 100 *céntimos*. The fractions of the money are the 5 and 10 *céntimos* pieces, and the 25 *céntimos* pieces or *reales* (by analogy the Spaniards call all sums of 25 *céntimos* a *real* as we call twenty-one shillings one guinea). The multiples are the five *pesetas* coin or *duro* of about the same size and appearance as a half-crown and the notes worth 5, 25, 50, 100, 500 and 1,000 *pesetas*.

The coinage and notes are made by the *Fábrica Nacional de Moneda y Timbre*, which produces also the postage stamps, cheques, etc., and the tickets for the National Lottery, for

which there is a *sorteo* (draw) twice a month bringing in a large income to the State.

The most usual abbreviations are : *pta(s).* for *peseta(s)*, *Kg(s).* for *kilogramo(s)*, *m./mts.* for *metro(s)*, *l./lts.* for *litro(s)*.

COINAGE, WEIGHTS, MEASURES	MONEDAS, PESAS, MEDIDAS
Vocabulary	Vocabulario
The money	El dinero
The change	El cambio
The small cash	La calderilla
The note	El billete
The Pound Sterling	La libra esterlina
The shilling	El chelín
The penny	El penique
The foreign currency	Las divisas
The peseta	La peseta
The centime	El céntimo
The five-pesetas piece	La moneda de cinco pesetas, el duro
The 25-centimes piece	El real
The 10-centimes coin	Diez céntimos (vulg. perra gorda)
The 5-centimes coin	Cinco céntimos (vulg. perra chica)
Weights :	Pesos :
the pound	la libra
the ounce	la onza
the hundredweight	el quintal
the ton	la tonelada
the gram	el gramo
the kilogram	el kilogramo
the hectogram	el hectogramo
the 25-lb. weight	la arroba
the scales	la balanza
to weigh	pesar

Linear Measures :	Medidas de longitud :
the millimetre	el milímetro
the centimetre	el centímetro
the metre	el metro
the kilometre	el kilómetro
the inch	la pulgada
the foot	el pie (lineal)
the yard	la yarda
the mile	la milla
the league	la legua
the ruler	la regla, el metro
the tape measure	la cinta métrica
to measure	medir
high	alto
wide	ancho
long	largo
deep	hondo
Liquid measures :	Medidas para líquidos :
the litre	el litro
the hectolitre	el hectólitro
the gallon	el galón
the pint	la pinta, el cuartillo
Square measures :	Medidas agrarias :
the square yard	la yarda cuadrada
the acre	el acre (aprox. 0,4 hectáreas)
the square metre	el metro cuadrado
the 100 square metres, the area	el área
the hectare	la hectárea
Cubic measures :	Medidas cúbicas :
the cubic metre	el metro cúbico
the cubic inch	la pulgada cúbica

Phrases	Frases
Can you lend me ten pesetas fifty ?	¿ Podría prestarme diez cincuenta ?
I have no change on me	No llevo cambio

Can I borrow a pound till to-morrow?	¿ Podría prestarme una libra esterlina hasta mañana ?
I have only a little silver	Tengo sólo un poco de plata
Are there copper coins in Spain?	¿ Hay monedas de cobre en España ?
No. The small cash is made of a tin alloy	No. La calderilla es de una aleación de estaño
Put a 10-centimes piece in the slot	Inserte una moneda de diez céntimos en la ranura
I have lost a 100-peseta note	He perdido un billete de cien pesetas
I have to pay 2,000 pesetas	Tengo que pagar dos mil pesetas
When can you repay me?	¿ Cuándo podrá devolvérmelas ?
He has run into debt	Ha contraído deudas
What do I owe you?	¿ Qué le debo ?
He is a black marketeer	Es estraperlista
Have you paid your income tax?	¿ Ha pagado usted su impuesto de utilidades ?
It is deducted from my salary	Lo deducen de mi sueldo
Did you weigh yourself on the platform scales?	¿ Se ha pesado usted en la báscula ?
My weight is 10 stones	Peso setenta kilos
How many pounds of oranges do you want me to buy?	¿ Cuántos kilos de naranjas quiere que compre ?
Two kilograms will be enough	Con dos kilos basta
How much is the ton of coal?	¿ Cuánto cuesta la tonelada de carbón ?
We have bought 50 lbs. of potatoes	Hemos comprado dos arrobas de patatas
A hundredweight of wheat	Un quintal de trigo
How far is Seville from Madrid?	¿ Qué distancia hay de Madrid a Sevilla ?
I was driving at 50 kilometres an hour	Iba yo conduciendo a cincuenta kilómetros por hora
Let me have 3 metres and 40 centimetres of this ribbon	Hágame el favor de tres metros cuarenta centímetros de esta cinta

The garden is 35 metres long and 20 metres wide	El jardín tiene treinta y cinco metros de largo por veinte de ancho
Will you take my measurements for a suit?	¿ Querría tomarme las medidas para un traje ?
These shoes are made to measure	Estos zapatos están hechos a la medida
Have you a tape measure to measure the length of this cloth?	¿ Tiene un metro para medir el largo de esta pieza de tela ?
Does your ruler show inches and centimetres?	¿ Tiene su regla pulgadas y centímetros ?
How many miles is it from San Sebastián to Barcelona?	¿ Cuántas millas hay de San Sebastián a Barcelona ?
I don't know the figure in miles, only in kilometres, but I will work it out presently	No sé la cifra en millas, sino en kilómetros, pero haré el cálculo en seguida
Half a pint of milk, please	Un cuarto de litro de leche
I have ordered 2 cubic metres of wood	He encargado dos metros cúbicos de leña

THE HUMAN BODY

Spaniards have a Social Insurance Scheme, called *Seguro de Enfermedad*, which is similar to the British Health Service, but it is available only to those who work (*productores*) and their immediate families.

All general services are covered, e.g., surgical operations, teeth extraction and so on, but not other forms of dentistry, or the free issue of spectacles, wigs, etc.

All State medical services are controlled by a State organisation called *Dirección General de Sanidad*. One of its most

important branches is the *Patronato Nacional Anti-tuberculoso*, which has about 20,000 beds at its disposal.

According to the latest statistics, the annual mortality rate is 9·5 per thousand, while the infantile mortality rate is 54 per thousand.

Apart from organisations controlled more or less by the State, there are, of course, doctors in private practice. In big towns there are private medical societies which have a panel of specialists at the service of members.

For the poorer classes there are free beds in hospitals run by nuns and *enfermeros* (male nurses).

One characteristic feature in Spanish towns is the *Casa de Socorro* (a kind of First Aid post), which is recognised at once by its red (or white) lamp and its red cross at the door. There is always a doctor on duty, with a policeman and a First Aid man. Here people who have suffered from an accident in the street or elsewhere are attended to, if necessary, while they wait for the ambulance to come and take them to the hospital.

THE HUMAN BODY— HEALTH

EL CUERPO HUMANO— LA SALUD

AT THE DOCTOR'S, AT THE DENTIST'S

EN CASA DEL MÉDICO, EN CASA DEL DENTISTA

Vocabulary

Vocabulario

The head	La cabeza
The face	La cara
The skull	El cráneo
The forehead	La frente
The eye	El ojo
The eyelid	El párpado
The eyebrow	La ceja
The eyelashes	Las pestañas
The ear	La oreja
The nose	La nariz
The mouth	La boca
The lip	El labio

The cheek	La mejilla
The chin	La barbilla
The jaw	La mandíbula
The tooth	El diente
The gum	La encía
The tongue	La lengua
The neck	El cuello
The throat	La garganta
The tonsil	La amígdala
The gland	La glándula
The hair	El pelo
The skin	La piel, el cutis
The trunk	El tronco
The bone	El hueso
The rib	La costilla
The spine	La espina dorsal
The chest	El pecho
The abdomen	El abdomen
The belly	El vientre
The lung	El pulmón
The heart	El corazón
The stomach	El estómago
The bowels	Los intestinos
The liver	El hígado
The kidney	El riñón
The shoulder	El hombro
The arm	El brazo
The elbow	El codo
The hand	La mano
The wrist	La muñeca
The finger	El dedo
The thumb	El pulgar
The small finger	El meñique
The nail	La uña
The thigh	El muslo
The leg	La pierna
The knee	La rodilla

The ankle	El tobillo
The foot	El pie
The toe	El dedo del pie
The sole	La planta del pie
The blood	La sangre
The vein	La vena
The blood circulation	La circulación de la sangre
The blood pressure	La presión sanguínea, la tensión
The illness, disease	La enfermedad
The hygiene	La higiene
The nutrition	La nutrición, la alimentación
The food	El alimento
The malnutrition	La desnutrición
The pain	El dolor
The headache	El dolor de cabeza
The sore throat	El dolor de garganta
The cold	El resfriado
The 'flu	La gripe
The catarrh	El catarro
The cough	La tos
The inflammation	La inflamación
The pneumonia	La pulmonía
The gastric trouble	Los trastornos gástricos
The tuberculosis	La tuberculosis
The bruise	El golpe, la magulladura
The cut	La cortadura
The fracture	La fractura
The medical examination	El reconocimiento médico
The treatment	El tratamiento
The medicine	La medicina
The prescription	La receta
The injection	La inyección
The ambulance	La ambulancia
The nurse	El enfermero/la enfermera
The hospital	El hospital
The ward	La sala
The microbe	El microbio

The blood test	El análisis de sangre
The analysis	El análisis
The toothache	El dolor de muelas
To anæsthetise	Anestesiar
To extract	Extraer
To fill	Empastar
To clean	Limpiar
To cure, to heal	Curar, cicatrizar
Contagious	Contagioso, infeccioso
To contaminate	Contaminar
Convalescent	Convaleciente
Healthy	Sano, saludable

Phrases	Frases
What are Dr. Redondo's consultation hours?	¿ Qué horas de consulta tiene el Dr. Redondo ?
Send for a doctor	Mande a buscar un médico
Do you want the practitioner or a specialist?	¿ Quiere el médico de cabecera o un especialista ?
Did you consult a surgeon for an operation?	¿ Ha consultado a un cirujano respecto a una operación ?
What is the matter with you?	¿ Qué es lo que le ocurre ?
I don't feel well	No me encuentro bien
I feel very ill	Me siento muy mal
I feel sick	Me dan náuseas
I feel giddy	Estoy mareado/a
I feel weak	Me siento débil
You have a sore throat	Tiene usted la garganta mal
Your tonsils are swollen	Tiene hinchadas las amígdalas
I am hoarse	Estoy ronco/a
I have caught a cold	He cogido un resfriado
I keep sneezing and coughing	No paro de estornudar y de toser
You must gargle and take a cough mixture	Tiene usted que hacer gárgaras y tomar un jarabe
Stay in bed for some days and take your temperature regularly	Quédese en cama por unos días y tómese la temperatura con regularidad

D

You are feverish, put the thermometer under your tongue	Tiene usted fiebre ; póngase el termómetro bajo la lengua
The temperature is going up (down)	La temperatura sube (baja)
Your pulse is very irregular	Su pulso es muy irregular
My heart is very weak	Mi corazón está muy débil
He is suffering from pneumonia (pleurisy, typhoid)	Está enfermo de pulmonía (pleuresía, fiebre tifoidea)
You must be taken to hospital	Hay que trasladarle a usted al hospital
I prefer a private clinic	Prefiero una clínica particular
The patient must not be disturbed	No se moleste al paciente
What are the fees for a visit to a nose, throat or ear specialist ?	¿ Cuáles son los honorarios de un especialista de garganta, nariz y oídos, por una consulta ?
I shall have to give you a thorough examination	Tendré que hacerle un reconocimiento a fondo
We shall have to take an X-ray	Habrá que hacerle una radiografía
Is your digestion all right?	¿ Digiere usted bien ?
The medicine was no good	La medicina no sirvió para nada
Take these pills and a teaspoonful of this powder after meals	Tome estas píldoras y una cucharadita de estos polvos después de las comidas
Shake the bottle	Agítese antes de usarlo
For external use only	Uso externo
Poison	Veneno
You have broken your arm	Se ha roto usted un brazo
We have to keep your leg in plaster	Tenemos que escayolarle la pierna
He has fractured his skull	Se ha fracturado el cráneo
You have had a bad concussion	Ha tenido una conmoción seria
I am injured	Estoy herido/a

Have you sprained your ankle?	¿ Se ha torcido un tobillo ?
You are badly bruised	Está usted lleno/a de contusiones
The illness got worse (better)	La enfermedad fué a peor (mejor)
The cut is healed but you can see the scar	La cortadura ha cicatrizado, pero queda la cicatriz
I must dress your wounds	Tengo que vendar sus heridas
I cannot hear well	No oigo bien
He is deaf and dumb	Es sordo-mudo
Your middle-ear is inflamed	Tiene usted inflamado el oído medio
I am short-sighted (long-sighted)	Soy miope (présbita)
Do you know a good oculist ?	¿ Sabe usted de un buen oculista ?
He is blind	Él es ciego
I need a pair of spectacles (glasses)	Necesito unas gafas (unos lentes)
He squints a little	Bizquea un poco
At the dentist's :	En el dentista :
Please come into the surgery	Haga el favor de pasar a la clínica
This back tooth (front tooth) hurts me	Me duele esta muela (este colmillo)
This tooth must be stopped	Hay que empastar este diente
The gums are bleeding	Le sangran las encías
I shall give you a local anæsthetic	Tengo que anestesiarle el nervio
The root is decayed	La raíz está cariada
Can't you manage without drilling ?	¿ No podría prescindir del barreno ?
The tooth must be extracted	Hay que sacar el diente
I have a gumboil	Tengo un flemón

What sort of mouth-wash (tooth-paste) do you use?	¿ Qué clase de enjuague (pasta dentífrica) usa usted ?
I am afraid you must have a denture	Creo que tiene que usar dentadura postiza
You must have a gold-crown on your teeth	Hay que ponerle una corona de oro
I shall have to get a new tooth-brush	Tendré que comprar otro cepillo de dientes
Is the treatment finished?	¿ Está terminado el tratamiento ?

AT THE HAIRDRESSER'S

Over the door of most barber's shops in Spain you will see a gilt-metal dish very much like the one which Don Quixote took for Mambrino's helmet. Beaumarchais' barber from Seville, who revelled in gossip and skill, is not too unlike the Spanish barber of to-day.

But the traditional barber's shop is gradually being replaced in the big cities by the modern *salón de peluquería* with its row of attendants (*oficiales*) and its up-to-date service for masculine hygiene, and by the *instituto de belleza* (Beauty Salon), which includes women's hairdressing as well as manicure, facial massage and so on.

These hairdressing establishments (*peluquerías*) remain open on Saturdays and often on Sunday mornings, but close one day in the week, usually on Mondays.

It is interesting to note that, in spite of his thick and dark beard, a Spaniard does not normally shave every day.

A large number of women who have dark eyes and eyebrows do not hesitate to join the legion of the " bottle blondes " (*rubias del frasco*), or " peroxide blondes " (*rubias oxigenadas*).

Incidentally, women are classed according to the colour of their hair as *morenas* (brunettes), *castañas* (chestnut-coloured), *rubias* (blondes) and *pelirrojas* or *azafranadas* (red-heads).

AT THE HAIRDRESSER'S	EN LA PELUQUERÍA
Vocabulary	Vocabulario
The gentlemen's hairdresser's	La peluquería de caballeros
The barber's shop	La barbería
The chiropodist	El callista
The safety razor	La maquinilla de afeitar
The safety razor blade	La hoja de afeitar
The razor blade	La navaja de afeitar
The shaving-brush	La brocha de afeitar
The shaving-lotion	La loción para el afeitado
The shaving-stick	La barra de jabón de afeitar
The tube of lather (brushless) shaving-cream	El tubo de crema de afeitar (sin brocha)
The hair-cream	El fijador
The eau de cologne	El agua de colonia
The hair-cut	El corte de pelo
The beard	La barba
The moustache	El bigote
To shave	Afeitar
To cut	Cortar
To trim	Recortar
To lather	Enjabonar
The ladies' hairdresser's	La peluquería de señoras
The manicure	La manicura
The perm(anent wave)	La (ondulación) permanente
The wave	La onda
The curl	El rizo, el bucle
The bun	El moño
The parting	La raya
The wash	El lavado de pelo
The hair-style	El peinado
The shampoo	El champú
The hair-net	La redecilla para el pelo
The hairpin	La horquilla
The curler	El rizador
The curling tongs	Las tenacillas

The comb	El peine
The hairbrush	El cepillo para el pelo
The perfume	El perfume
The nail varnish	El esmalte para las uñas
The talcum powder	Los polvos de talco
The face powder	Los polvos para la cara
The lipstick	La barra de los labios
The tweezers	Las pinzas
To set the waves	Marcar las ondas
To dry	Secar
To dye (grey hair)	Teñir (las canas)
To bleach	Decolorar
To massage	Dar masaje

Phrases

Frases

Is there a gentleman's hairdresser near here?	¿ Hay alguna peluquería de caballeros por aquí cerca ?
How do you want it, sir?	¿ Qué va a ser ?
A haircut, please, short sides and back	Corte de pelo, corto por los lados y de atrás
Not too short, please	No me lo deje muy corto
A two-days-old beard	Una barba de dos días
Please trim my moustache	Recórteme el bigote
I should like a shampoo	Quisiera que me lavase el pelo con champú
You can give me a shave, too	Haga el favor de afeitarme también
Does this shaving-cream make a good lather?	¿ Suelta mucha espuma esta crema de afeitar ?
Here is a hot towel, sir	Aquí tiene una toalla caliente, señor
He is getting bald	Está quedando calvo
He is turning grey	Están saliéndole canas
Have you a hair-restorer?	¿ Tiene alguna loción capilar ?
Have you any good hair-oil?	¿ Tiene una buena brillantina ?
Should I leave a tip for the hairdresser's assistant?	¿ Tengo que darle propina al aprendiz ?

I would like to make an appointment with my usual assistant for to-morrow at eleven	Desearía quedar de acuerdo con mi peluquero/a de costumbre para mañana a las once
Everything is booked up for to-morrow, I am sorry	Lo siento, pero mañana tengo todo el día comprometido
Can I come for a perm on Monday?	¿ Puedo venir el lunes a hacerme la permanente ?
Don't cut off too much, please	Por favor, no me corte demasiado
I want curls at the back	Quisiera el pelo todo rizado por atrás
I should like to try a new hair-style	Quisiera probar un estilo nuevo de peinado
What colour do you want your hair dyed?	¿ En qué color quiere teñirse el pelo ?
I should like a copper shade	Me gustaría un tono caoba
Do you sell lipsticks and nail varnish to match?	¿ Venden barras de los labios y esmalte para las uñas haciendo juego ?
For your make-up we have cream and face powder, eyebrow pencils and rouge	Para el maquillaje tenemos cremas y polvos de la cara, lápices para las cejas y carmín
Have you a manicure and pedicure service here?	¿ Tienen servicio de manicura y pedicuro ?
There is a chiropodist next door	En la casa de al lado hay un callista
Have you any bath salts and toilet soap?	¿ Tienen sales de baño y jabón de tocador ?

CLOTHING

Textiles from Cataluña and footwear from the Balearic Islands are world-renowned for their quality. This fact, added to their comparatively low price, encourages tourists to spend their last *pesetas* on textiles. The French call this the *opération gabardine*. There is not a corresponding *opération* for footwear, because Spanish shoe shapes do not usually fit the feet of other Europeans.

Spanish women prefer to wear high heels rather than the modern low sports heels.

A Spaniard considers it as important to wear well-polished shoes as an Englishman does to shave every day; and everywhere, in the streets and in cafés, you will find *limpiabotas* (shoe cleaners) at their work.

Even though the Catalan factories make well-cut ready-made suits, the Spaniard prefers to have his made to measure. Tailoring is cheap but good, although the style differs slightly from the English. At present Spanish tailors seem to cut their suits after the American style rather than the English.

Women are even more averse to wearing ready-made garments. Many make their own, and, if not, they go to one of the many dressmakers, who, incidentally, charge little for their skilled work.

Perhaps because of the abundant sunlight Spanish women do not wear as bright colours as their English sisters. Most women prefer smart suits and dresses in black. This is also due to the fact that people go into mourning more readily and for a longer time than in England.

Although in everyday life hats are not often worn, they are brought out on all special occasions.

CLOTHING	EL VESTUARIO
Vocabulary	Vocabulario
Men's Clothes :	Las Prendas de Hombre :
The pyjamas	El pijama
The dressing-gown	La bata

The slippers	Las zapatillas
The socks	Los calcetines
The shoe	El zapato
The suspenders, garters	Las ligas
The drawers, pants	Los calzoncillos
The vest	La camiseta
The shirt	La camisa
The braces	Los tirantes
The belt	El cinturón
The collar	El cuello
The stud	El pasador del cuello
The cuff-links	Los gemelos
The tie	La corbata
The suit	El traje
The jacket	La chaqueta, la americana
The trousers	El pantalón
The waistcoat	El chaleco
The lounge-suit	El traje de calle
The dinner-jacket	El smoking
The tail-coat, " tails "	El frac
The overcoat	El abrigo
The cap	La gorra visera
The hat	El sombrero
The beret	La boina
The gloves	Los guantes
The stick	El bastón
The umbrella	El paraguas
The scarf	La bufanda
The handkerchief	El pañuelo
The raincoat	El impermeable
The cut length	El corte de traje
Women's Clothes :	Las Prendas de Mujer :
The stockings	Las medias
The underwear	La ropa interior
The brassiere	El sostén
The slip	La combinación, la enagua

The brief	La braga
The night-dress	El camisón
The girdle, roll-on	La faja
The dress, gown	El vestido, el traje
The evening-dress	El traje de noche
The blouse	La blusa
The coat and skirt	El traje sastre
The apron	El delantal, el mandil
The sports wear	El conjunto de deporte
The cardigan	La chaqueta de punto
The pull-over	El jersey
The fur coat	El abrigo de pieles
The veil	El velo
The mantilla	La mantilla
The square	El pañuelo del cuello, la bufanda
The Manila mantle	El mantón de Manila
The shawl	El chal
The fashion	La moda
The design	El modelo
The material	El tejido, la tela
The silk	La seda
The velvet	El terciopelo
The wool	La lana
The linen	El lino
The coat-hanger	La percha
The court-shoe	El zapato de tacón alto
The walking-shoe	El zapato de calle
The jewels, jewelry	Las joyas
The ring	El anillo
The necklace	El collar
The bracelet	La pulsera
The earrings	Los pendientes
The tailor	El sastre
The dressmaker	El modisto, la modista
The milliner	La sombrerera
To dress	Vestirse
To undress	Desnudarse

To take off (a garment, a hat)	Quitarse (una prenda, un sombrero)
To put on (a garment, shoes, etc.)	Ponerse (una prenda, los zapatos, etc.)
To sew	Coser
To mend	Remendar, arreglar
To darn	Zurcir
Red	Rojo, roja—encarnado, encarnada
Blue	Azul
Green	Verde
Yellow	Amarillo, amarilla
Brown	Castaño, marrón, color café
Grey	Gris
Black	Negro, negra
White	Blanco, blanca
Purple	Morado, morada
Maroon	Granate
Light and dark	Claro y oscuro
Silver	De plata
Golden	De oro

Phrases	Frases
Have you a good tailor?	¿ Tiene usted un buen sastre ?
I want a suit made to measure	Desearía un traje hecho a la medida
I prefer it to a ready-made one	Lo prefiero a uno de confección
What sort of material do you stock?	¿ Qué clase de tejidos tiene ?
I want a lounge-suit	Desearía un traje de calle
Single-breasted or double-breasted?	¿ De una fila o cruzado ?
Please line the pockets with chamois-leather	Tenga la bondad de ponerme los forros de los bolsillos de piel de gamuza
Do you wear braces or a belt?	¿ Usa usted tirantes o cinturón ?

The sleeves are too short	Las mangas son cortas
The trousers are too long	El pantalón es largo
The lapels are too wide	Las solapas son muy anchas
The jacket does not fit	La chaqueta no me sienta
To-morrow is your first fitting	Mañana se le hará la primera prueba
I should like a dark sports jacket and a pair of light flannel trousers	Desearía una chaqueta oscura de sport y pantalón claro de franela
The suit is well cut	El traje tiene buen corte
Show me some check shirts, please	Haga el favor de enseñarme camisas a cuadros
Six starched collars	Seis cuellos almidonados(duros)
Have you a blue silk tie?	¿ Tiene corbatas azules de seda ?
Half a dozen coloured and a dozen white handkerchiefs	Media docena de pañuelos de color y una docena blancos
The hat is too big for me	El sombrero me está demasiado grande
I must send my grey hat to be cleaned	Tengo que mandar a limpiar el sombrero gris
This suit must be repaired, the lining is torn	Hay que mandar a arreglar este traje ; tiene el forro roto
Please send these shoes to be half-soled	Haga el favor de mandar estos zapatos a que les pongan medias suelas
The slippers need new heels	Las zapatillas necesitan tacones nuevos
I like plain socks	Me gustan los calcetines de colores lisos
The woollen socks have shrunk	Los calcetines de lana han encogido
The colours have run	Los colores se han corrido
Do you prefer brown or black shoes?	De qué color prefiere los zapatos : ¿ marrón o negros ?
The shoes are too narrow	Los zapatos me están estrechos
The toe-caps of these boots pinch	Las punteras de estas botas me lastiman

A pair of brown laces, please	Unos cordones marrón, por favor
Which lasts longer, silk or nylon underwear?	Cuál dura más: ¿la ropa interior de seda o la de nailon?
Have you any pink slips which are not too expensive?	¿Tienen combinaciones de color rosa que no sean muy caras?
Where can I get the ladders of my stockings repaired?	¿Dónde me pueden coger los puntos de las medias?
They have three ladders and some holes, too	Tienen tres carreras y algunos agujeros, además
I want a blue-striped blouse with long sleeves	Desearía una blusa a rayas azules y de manga larga
The brown skirt is very smart	La falda color café es muy elegante
It is too large for me	Me está demasiado grande
You can have it altered	Se le puede arreglar
Could you show me some silk afternoon dresses?	¿Podría enseñarme trajes de tarde de seda?
I need a light woollen winter-dress	Necesito un vestido de invierno de lanilla
Have you any autumn wear?	¿Tienen trajes de entretiempo para el otoño?
Have you any low-necked evening-dresses?	¿Tienen ustedes trajes de noche de mucho escote?
I want a black-laced veil	Desearía un velo de encaje negro
This green morning-gown is very becoming	Ese salto de cama verde la cae muy bien
This cardigan is nice and warm	Esta chaqueta de punto abriga bastante
In that shop you can find leather goods and suede gloves	En esa tienda encontrará usted objetos de cuero y guantes de ante
I need a new handbag with a purse and a wallet	Necesito un bolsillo nuevo con monedero y cartera para los billetes (de banco)

I am looking for a pair of shoes size five	Ando buscando un par de zapatos número cinco
I am sorry, madam, in Spain sizes are numbered differently. Yours is number 35, I dare say	Lo siento, señora, la numeración en España es diferente. Yo diría que su tamaño es el treinta y cinco
This hat with black feathers does not match my brown coat	Este sombrero de plumas negras no hace juego con mi abrigo marrón
I will take this silver wristwatch with a leather strap	Me quedaré con este reloj de pulsera de plata que tiene la correa de cuero
Have you any small golden earrings?	¿Tienen pendientes pequeños de oro?

THE THEATRE

Foreigners do not, as a rule, get much pleasure from contemporary Spanish plays, but if they are interested in the works of Calderón, Lope de Vega, etc., they can see them performed in theatres patronised by the State. There are two performances daily, the first at 7.30 p.m., the second at 10.30 p.m., Sundays included.

Apart from plays, *cuadros folklóricos* are very popular. These are shows put on by companies which include dancers, singers guitar players, etc. Sometimes there is a slight plot running through, but more often than not, they consist of a series of independent " turns " which bring to the stage the national folklore for which Spain is so famous. More authentic shows, of this type, are the *juergas* performed in *colmaos* (taverns) where the audience can drink *manzanilla* (a type of sherry) while watching the acts. The caves of the Sacro-Monte in Granada—the home of the Spanish gypsies—often echo to the sound of these *juergas*.

The *zarzuela*, a kind of Spanish " musical " or opera, is also popular.   This usually represents some local custom or event, and is really an excuse for the introduction of arias, duets and choruses of Hispanic origin.

Every theatre has its own bar, where coffee, drinks and snacks (but *not* tea) are served.

The audience shows its appreciation by ordinary applause, never by whistling.   Spanish actors always get a shock when they hear themselves being whistled in England.   The Spaniards show their displeasure by silence, and only very rarely by stamping and whistling.   Silence is sufficient for the Spanish actor !

The prompter does not sit in a corner, but in the *concha*, which is a shell-shaped structure in the very middle of the front of the stage.

Only in the biggest cities do you find permanent circuses. In the other places the circus arrives usually during the local fair and performs in the outskirts of the town in a shed (tent) of wood and canvas.

THE THEATRE AND OTHER ENTERTAINMENTS	EL TEATRO Y OTROS ESPECTÁCULOS
Vocabulary	Vocabulario
The entertainments guide	La cartelera de espectáculos
The play	La obra
The curtain-raiser	El entremés
The comedy	La comedia
The tragedy	La tragedia
The drama	El drama
The musical	La opereta
The variety show	La compañía de variedades
The revue	La revista
The Spanish popular musical	La zarzuela
The Spanish Folkloric show	El cuadro flamenco
The Andalusian folk songs	El cante jondo

The dance	El baile, la danza
The circus	El circo
The public	El público
The seating capacity	El aforo
The late-night performance	La función de la noche
The early evening performance	La función de la tarde
The foyer	El vestíbulo
The cloakroom	El tocador
The refreshment room	El bar
The auditorium	La sala
The box	El palco
The stalls	Las butacas
The dress circle	El entresuelo
The upper circle	El anfiteatro
The gallery	El gallinero
The pit	El foso de la orquesta
The stage	El escenario, el tablado
The footlights	Las candilejas
The fly	La bambalina
The wings	Los bastidores
The dressing-room	El camerino
The prompter's box	La concha
The scenery	Los decorados
The background	El foro
The prompter	El apuntador
The props-man	El tramoyista
The theatre company	La compañía de teatro
The show company	La compañía de revistas
The company	El conjunto
The producer	El director de escena
The author	El autor
The playwright	El autor dramático, el dramaturgo
The poet	El poeta
The cast	El reparto
The actor, actress	El actor, la actriz

The leading man	El primer actor
The leading lady	La primera actriz
The dancer	El bailarín, la bailarina
The dance partners	La pareja de baile
The singer	El (la) cantante
The songstress	La cupletista
The flamenco singer	El cantador de flamenco
The understudy	El sustituto, la sustituta
The acrobat	El acróbata
The conjurer	El prestidigitador
The clown	El payaso
The tamer	El domador de fieras
The scene	La escena
The part	El papel
The aside	El aparte
The finale	El cuadro final
The actor's exit	El mutis
The interval	El entreacto
The fire curtain	El telón de acero
The applause	El aplauso
The booing	El pateo
To tour	Hacer une tournée
To tour the provinces	Salir a provincias
To watch a performance	Asistir a una representación

Phrases	Frases
What is on at the theatre, to-day?	¿ Qué ponen hoy en el teatro ?
A drama by a modern author at the State Theatre	Un drama de un autor moderno, en el teatro " Español "
We shall not get any tickets	No vamos a poder conseguir localidades
The house is sold out	Está todo vendido
Can I order tickets by telephone?	¿ Puedo encargar billetes por teléfono ?
Can you see well from that seat?	¿ Puede usted ver bien desde ese asiento ?

I need opera-glasses	Necesito prismáticos
I would like some coffee in the interval	Quisiera tomar café en el entreacto
You can only have it in the refreshment room	Solamente lo puede tomar en el bar
The curtain rises (falls)	Se levanta (cae) el telón
The première of this play has been postponed	El estreno de esta obra ha sido aplazado
What a magnificent stage setting !	¡ Qué puesta en escena más formidable !
This young leading lady has a great future	Esta joven primera actriz tiene gran porvenir
The main character has not learned his part well	El protagonista no se sabe el papel bien
The play is enthralling (boring) (amusing)	La obra es emocionante (aburrida) (divertida)
The footlights are too bright	Las candilejas son demasiado fuertes
The performance was booed	La representación fué pateada
The applause was frantic (feeble)	Aplaudieron frenéticamente (sin entusiasmo)
Did you see the couple of Spanish dancers in the new folkloric show?	¿ Ha visto usted la pareja de baile española en el nuevo cuadro flamenco ?
The guitarist is a gipsy from Andalusia	El guitarrista es un gitano de Andalucía
The songs of this musical are by a well-known composer	Las canciones de esta opereta son de un compositor muy conocido
I would like to take the children to the circus	Quisiera llevar los niños al circo
Have they enjoyed the performance?	¿ Les ha gustado la función ?

OPERAS AND CONCERTS

Except in those big towns where concerts are gradually rivalling in number and quality those of any other important European city, Spanish towns usually rely on the local branch of the "Philharmonic Society" to provide musical evenings. This Society has branches all over the Iberian Peninsula, and, in return for a small subscription, manages to offer its members once or twice a month concerts in which musicians of international repute take part.

Every town has its own municipal band, which usually plays in the morning in the bandstand in a park. In the north of Spain there are also plenty of choral societies.

Spain is very rich in musical folklore, which ranges from Andalusian melodies, obviously inspired by Moorish music, to the sentimental and nostalgic songs of Galicia with their undeniable Celtic flavour.

Spain is in fact a land of song : men sing while they shave, women while they iron, and the courtyards of dwelling-houses always echo with songs sung by the occupants as they go about their daily work.

The opera does not appear to flourish so much in Spain as in England, France or the U.S.A. At present the "Covent Garden" of Spain is the Teatro Liceo in Barcelona, although performances are also given sometimes in the Capital at the Teatro Madrid. The future home of the opera in Spain will be in Madrid at the Teatro Real, which is still under reconstruction.

THE OPERA AND THE CONCERT-HALL
Vocabulary

LA OPERA Y LA SALA DE CONCIERTOS
Vocabulario

The gala performance	La función de gala
The benefit	La función benéfica
The concert	El concierto
The recital	El recital
The music	La música
The libretto	El libreto

The score	La partitura
The composer	El compositor
The soprano	La tiple
The tenor	El tenor
The baritone	El barítono
The bass	El bajo
The aria	El aria
The duet	El dúo
The chorus	El coro
The figurant	El comparsa
The ballet	El ballet
The conductor	El director de orquesta
The orchestra	La orquesta
The musician	El músico
The baton	La batuta
The soloist	El solista
The first violin	El primer violín
The bass-violin	El violón
The cello	El violoncelo
The (grand) piano	El piano (de cola)
The flute	La flauta
The drum	El tambor
The harp	El arpa
The trumpet	La trompeta
The chamber music	La música de cámara
The choir	El coro
The song	La canción
The sonata	La sonata
The symphony	La sinfonía
To play an instrument	Tocar un instrumento
To beat the time	Marcar el tiempo
To listen to the music	Escuchar la música
To bow	Saludar

Phrases

Frases

Here are two tickets for to-night's concert

Aquí tiene dos localidades para el concierto de esta noche

Who is conducting?	¿ Quién dirige ?
An Italian conductor	Un director de orquesta italiano
Do you prefer classical or modern music?	Qué música prefiere : ¿ la clásica o la moderna ?
I have been listening to the light music played by the municipal band	He estado escuchando la música ligera que tocaba la banda municipal
Do you like chamber-music?	¿ Le gusta la música de cámara?
The soloist is a famous soprano (contralto)	La solista es una soprano (contralto) famosa
This opera has a ballet in the second act	Esta ópera tiene un ballet en el segundo acto
All brass instruments are placed on the left of the stage	Todos los instrumentos de viento están situados a la izquierda del escenario
The third tempo of this symphony is based on string instruments	El tercer tiempo de esta sinfonía es a base de instrumentos de cuerda
After this there is a women's choir	A continuación hay un coro de voces blancas
To-morrow's gala performance is in the honour of a foreign composer	La función de gala de mañana será en honor de un compositor extranjero
Did you go to last night's recital of Modern Spanish music?	¿ Ha asistido usted al recital de anoche, de música española moderna ?

THE CINEMA

A few Spanish cinemas have continuous performances (*sesión continua*), but the majority have regular houses at fixed times, which means that seats can be booked hours or even days before. The tickets (*entradas*) have the number of the

row (*fila*) and the number of the seat (*butaca*), and no one is allowed to use your seat even if you do not go.

Performances are shorter than in England, and only very few have a double-feature programme. A special children's show (*programa infantil*) is sometimes given on Sunday or Thursday afternoons.

Smoking is strictly forbidden, but there is always a five-minute interval (*descanso*) for a smoke in the foyer or a drink in the bar. A bell is rung to announce the resumption of the performance.

There are a few Spanish films, but the majority are American, French or English. As the Spaniards go to hear and see, rather than to read subtitles to the film, dubbing is customary and is exceptionally well done. Each foreign film star has, as it were, a Spanish ghost who speaks for him. So do not be surprised to see, or rather hear, Sir Laurence Olivier, or Bob Hope, speaking with a pure Castilian accent !

In any case a visit to the cinema is a good exercise in comprehension of the Spanish language.

CINEMA	CINE
Vocabulary	Vocabulario
The cinema	El cine(matógrafo)
The local cinema	El cine del barrio
The film	La película, la cinta, el film
The screen	La pantalla
The talkie	La película sonora
The silent film	La película muda
The plot	El argumento
The cartoon	El film de dibujos (animados)
The news-reel	El noticiario
The Western	La película del Oeste
The detective film	La película policíaca
The slapstick comedy film	La película cómica
The documentary	El documental
The film studio	Los estudios cinematográficos
The projector	El proyector

The slides	Las diapositivas
The dubbing	El doblaje
The subtitles	Los rótulos
The cut	El corte
The sound-track	La banda sonora
The close-up	El primer plano
The script	El guión
The script writer	El guionista
The director	El director
The revival	El reestreno, la reprise
The re-make	La nueva versión
The cinema-goer	El espectador de cine
The cinema programmes	La cartelera
The double-feature programme	El programa doble
The supporting programme	Los complementos
The U-certificate film	La película tolerada para menores
The continuous performance	La sesión continua
The separate performances	El programa por sesiones
The doorman	El portero
The cashier	La taquillera
The booking desk, box office	La taquilla
The usher, usherette	El acomodador, la acomodadora
The projectionist	El operador
The choc-ice	El bombón helado
The sweets	Los caramelos
The film-fan	El aficionado al cine
The cast	El reparto
The hero	El protagonista
The female star	La estrella
The male star	El astro
The villain	El " malo "
The tough	El bruto
The glamour girl	La vampiresa
Mickey Mouse	El ratoncito Mickey
Donald Duck	El pato Donal

Charlie Chaplin	Charlot (Carlitos, in Latin-America)
The End	Fin
The anthem	El himno
To film	Filmar
To shoot	Rodar
To go to the pictures	Ir al cine

Phrases	Frases
When does the next performance start?	¿ Cuándo empieza la próxima sesión ?
The news-reel is shown at 3.30	El noticiario comienza a las tres treinta
Is this a continuous performance?	¿ Es sesión continua ?
When is the first-night of that film going to be?	¿ Cuándo va a ser el estreno de ese film ?
Look up the programmes in the evening papers	Lea los programas en la cartelera de los periódicos de la noche
Two central stalls for the last performance, please	Dos butacas del centro para la sesión de la noche
We had better sit at the back	Mejor nos sentamos en la parte de atrás
Is there any emergency exit?	¿ Hay por ahí alguna salida en caso de incendio ?
Can tickets be booked in advance?	¿ Pueden sacarse las entradas con anticipación ?
I know you know the plot, but please don't tell me	Ya sé que conoce usted el argumento, pero no me lo cuente
A new film is being shown	Ponen una película de estreno
I have seen this film before	Ya he visto este film
It's only a revival	Es nada más que reestreno
This comedy is very amusing but the film flickers	Esta comedia es muy divertida, pero la copia está rayada
Don't miss it !	¡ No te la pierdas !

They obtained the copyright of a famous novel for this script	Han comprado los derechos de una novela famosa para hacer este guión
Did you read the review on the technicolour musical?	¿ Ha leído usted la crítica sobre la revista en tecnicolor ?
I would like to see the dance sequel in slow motion	Me gustaría ver la secuencia de baile a cámara lenta
In which studio was this film shot?	¿ En qué estudios se rodó este film ?
The scene was shot on location	La escena está tomada del natural
This documentary is rather slow moving	Este documental es muy lento
Isn't this detective story thrilling !	¡ Qué emocionante es esta película policíaca !
The criminal is always the one you suspect the least	El criminal es siempre el que menos sospecha uno.

WIRELESS AND TELEVISION

There are more than one hundred official Broadcasting Stations in Spain ; the most important, R.N.E., i.e. *Radio Nacional de España*, whose News Bulletins are relayed through all the National Stations, broadcasts special programmes to Latin America.   Except for R.N.E., the other stations have the initials E.A.J., which were adopted at the International Congress, followed by a distinguishing number ; e.g., E.A.J. 34 stands for Gijón Broadcasting Station.

The programmes are very varied, and there is an epidemic of radio competitions, usually sponsored by commercial houses, who provide prizes of all kinds to the winners.

Sometimes there are competitions to bring out unknown artists, sometimes quizzes which consist in guessing the name of a tune (*la melodía misteriosa*) or answering a series of ques-

tions. Serials are very popular also, especially among the less-educated classes.

Before each item the announcers speak thus : " Now you will hear 'Ave María ', by Gounod " (*A continuación van ustedes a oír el Ave María de Gounod*) and, at the end, " You have just heard the 'Ave María ', by Gounod " (*Acaban de escuchar el "Ave María ", de Gounod*).

As in England, a licence is required before using a wireless set. This is obtained annually from the local *Delegación de Hacienda*.

WIRELESS AND TELEVISION
LA RADIO Y LA TELEVISIÓN

Vocabulary / Vocabulario

The broadcasting station	La (estación) emisora
The transmission	La emisión
The reception	La recepción
The wireless set, radio	El (aparato) receptor, la radio
The loudspeaker	El altavoz
The earphones	Los auriculares
The battery set	La batería
The valve	La válvula
The condenser	El condensador
The volume	El volúmen
The cabinet	La caja
The knobs	Los mandos
The mains	La red de consumo
The aerial	La antena
The frame aerial	La antena de cuadro
The inside aerial	La antena interior
The flex, wire	El flexible, el alambre
The adjustment	El ajuste
The direct current (D.C.)	La corriente continua
The alternating current (A.C.)	La corriente alterna
The disturbances, " atmospherics "	Los ruidos atmosféricos
The interference	Los parásitos

The short wave	La onda corta
The medium wave	La onda media
The long wave	La onda larga
The selectivity	La selectividad
The microphone	El micrófono
The announcer	El locutor
The programme parade	La lectura del programa
The disc, record	El disco
The news	Las noticias
The weather forecast	El boletín meteorológico
The serials	Las emisiones seriadas
The listener	El, la (radi) oyente
The television set	El aparato de televisión
The screen	El visor, la pantalla
To tune in	Sintonizar
To listen in	Escuchar
To earth	Poner a tierra
To switch on	Enchufar
To switch off	Desenchufar

Phrases / Frases

Can you pick up foreign stations with your set?	¿ Coge usted estaciones extranjeras con su aparato ?
I want to buy a four valve set	Quiero comprar una radio de cuatro válvulas
My set is out of order	Mi radio no funciona
The rectifying valve is fused	Se ha fundido la válvula rectificadora
My radio is subject to disturbances and fading	Mi receptor acusa las perturbaciones atmosféricas y la debilitación del sonido
The reception is poor	Se oye con dificultad
Can you recommend a good wireless repair shop?	¿ Podría recomendarme un buen taller de reparaciones de radios ?
Can you send someone round to have a look at it?	¿ Podría enviarme a alguien que le echase un vistazo ?

The valves should be renewed	Hay que ponerle válvulas nuevas
Where do I take out a licence for my set?	¿ Dónde he de sacar el permiso para mi radio ?
The licence is taken out at the local Finance Office	El permiso se saca en la Delegación local de Hacienda
Do you often listen in?	¿ Escucha usted con frecuencia la radio ?
Only when they broadcast concerts	Sólo cuando radian conciertos
Is there a lecture on the air to-night?	¿ Radian alguna conferencia esta noche ?
My neighbours' wireless disturbs me	Me molesta la radio de mis vecinos
I like to hear programmes of selected music	Me gusta oír los programas de música variada
Did you hear the news?	¿ Oyó usted las noticias ?
There is a radio-play to-night at eight	Esta noche a las ocho radian una obra de teatro
What was the weather forecast?	¿ Cómo fué el boletín meteorológico ?
Have you bought a television set in instalments?	¿ Ha comprado usted un aparato de televisión a plazos ?
The screen is very small	Tiene un visor muy pequeño
My neighbours come to my house to view the children's programme	Mis vecinos vienen a casa a ver el programa infantil
Would you like to listen to a broadcast of the Philharmonic Orchestra?	¿ Le gustaría escuchar una radiación de la Orquesta Filarmónica ?
The stations are closing down for to-night	Las estaciones están cerrando sus emisiones de esta noche
They always close with the national anthem	Cierran siempre con el himno nacional
One can hear the station signal	Se oye la señal de la estación

PHOTOGRAPHY

Although there is no actual manufacture or production of cameras and equipment in Spain, the people who develop or print are usually very competent.

There are plenty of studios where excellent modern photographs are taken for a comparatively moderate price.

The greatest difficulty encountered by the English photographer is the difference between the intensity of light in Spain and that in Great Britain. Without an exposure meter, considerable practice is required to compete with the sun of " sunny Spain ". The intensity of light, the variety and colour of the countryside and villages make Spain a colour-photographer's paradise.

PHOTOGRAPHY	LA FOTOGRAFIA
Vocabulary	**Vocabulario**
The camera	La cámara, el aparato fotográfico
The box camera	La cámara de cajón
The folding camera	La cámara plegable
The miniature camera	La cámara miniatura
The film	La película
The roll film	El rollo
The plate	La placa
The lens	La lente
The spool	El carrete
The aperture	La abertura
The diaphragm	El diafragma
The shutter	El obturador
The filter	El filtro
The flash	El flash
The self-timer	El autodisparador
The view finder	El visor
The exposure meter	La célula fotoeléctrica, el fotómetro
The leather case	La funda de cuero

The tripod	El trípode
The photograph	La foto(grafía)
The snapshot	La instantánea
The time exposure	La foto con exposición
The light	La luz
The focus	El foco
The stereoscopic photograph	La foto(grafía) estereoscópica
The colour photograph	La foto(grafía) en color
The three-dimensional film	La película en relieve
The negative	El negativo, el cliché
The positive	El positivo
The developer	El revelador
The fixer	El fijador
The print	La copia
The printing paper	El papel de copias
The dark room	La cámara oscura
The photographer	El fotógrafo
The street photographer	El fotógrafo ambulante
The cameraman	El cameraman
The objective	El objetivo
Under-exposed	Exposición escasa
Over-exposed	Exposición pasada
To expose	Exponer
To focus	Enfocar
To develop	Revelar
To enlarge	Ampliar
To retouch	Retocar
To make copies	Sacar copias

Phrases

Frases

May I take a photograph here?	¿Podría tomar aquí una foto?
You must hand in your camera	Tiene usted que depositar la cámara
Where can I get photographic materials?	¿Dónde puedo conseguir material fotográfico?
I want a roll film, size 6 by 9 cms.	Desearía un carrete de 6 por 9

Could you put it in for me?	¿ Tendría la bondad de ponérmelo ?
Do you develop plates and films?	¿ Hacen revelado de placas y carretes ?
Please let me have a proof	Haga el favor de facilitarme una copia
These photos are under-exposed	Estas fotos tienen exposición escasa
Could you intensify them?	¿ Podría intensificarlas ?
Is the light too bright for a time-exposure?	¿ Hay demasiada luz para una foto con exposición ?
I should like to have this snapshot enlarged	Quisiera que me ampliaran esta instantánea
How much would an enlargement cost?	¿ Cuánto costaría una ampliación ?
This portrait is out of focus	Este retrato está desenfocado
Can you recommend a good photographer?	¿ Puede usted recomendarme un buen fotógrafo ?
I am going to have my photo taken	Me voy a retratar
I shall keep the photographs in an album	Voy a guardar las fotos en un álbum
Have you bought a suitable frame for this landscape photo?	¿ Ha comprado usted un marco apropiado para esta foto de paisaje ?
Are you a keen photographer?	¿ Es usted aficionado(a) a la fotografía ?

SPORTS

It can truthfully be said that Spaniards indulge in every sport and play every game except cricket. Association football is undoubtedly the most popular; it is played, as in England, on a League and Cup basis, between teams from the

various Spanish towns. Some of the big grounds or stadiums (*estadios*), for instance, *Chamartín* and *Metropolitano* in Madrid or *Las Corts* and *Montjuich* in Barcelona, hold more than 50,000 people.

Athletic championships are held annually.

Winter sports enthusiasts in the North of Spain have plenty of opportunities on the surrounding mountains. Those in Barcelona can go to La Molina, whilst those in Madrid go to the Gredos or the Guadarrama mountains.

Because there are few indoor swimming-pools, swimming is rather a summer sport enjoyed mainly at the seaside. The three most important clubs are those of Cataluña, Madrid and the Canary Islands.

In summer, too, there are regattas for light craft, and fishing boats in the summer holiday resorts.

Salmon and trout are fished in the Northern rivers.

Andalusian horses are famous. In farms where bulls are bred there are usually excellent stables and hunts are often organised.

Lawn tennis is not so popular as in England; but clubs do exist, and a fair number of people play. Golf is even less popular, although foreigners have been introducing it little by little. Basket-ball and baseball are both growing in popularity.

Finally, Pelota, a game of Basque origin, which is a combination of our game of rackets, real tennis and fives, has a great following, especially in the Northern provinces of Spain. Its unique feature is a complicated betting system carried on in the *frontones* of the big towns.

GYMNASTICS AND ATHLETICS	GIMNASIA Y ATLETISMO
Vocabulary	Vocabulario
The cinder-track	La pista de ceniza
The gymnasium	El gimnasio
The gymnastic apparatus	Los aparatos de gimnasia
The trapeze	El trapecio

The rings	Las anillas
The ladder	La escala
The parallel bars	Las (barras) paralelas
The horse	El burro
The pole	La pértiga
The rope	La cuerda
The dumb-bells	Las palanquetas
The club	La clava, la maza
The spring-board	El trampolín
Swedish gymnastics	Gimnasia sueca
Rhythmics	Gimnasia rítmica
The high jump	El salto de altura
The long jump	El salto de longitud
The hop, skip and jump	El triple salto
The race	La carrera
The marathon	El maratón
The decathlon	El decatlón
The relay (race)	La carrera por relevos
The goal	La meta
The gym shorts	El pantalón de deporte
The plimsoles (gym shoes)	Las sandalias de gimnasia
The athlete	El atleta
To run	Correr
To jump	Saltar
To climb	Trepar
To bend the knees	Doblar las rodillas
To throw the discus (javelin, weight, hammer)	Lanzar el disco (la jabalina, el peso, el martillo)
To train	Entrenar(se)
To be fit	Estar en forma

Phrases / Frases

Do you do physical exercises in the morning?	¿ Hace usted ejercicio físico por la mañana ?
Are you going to take part in the thousand-metre race?	¿ Va usted a tomar parte en la carrera de los mil metros ?

E

I do not feel fit to take part in the four-hundred-metre hurdle championship	Me encuentro en baja forma para participar en la prueba de los cuatrocientos metros vallas
Have you a good trainer?	¿ Tiene usted un buen entrenador ?
Who has broken the long-jump record?	¿ Quién ha batido la marca del salto de longitud ?
Let's go and see the discus throwing	Vamos a ver el lanzamiento de disco
Can you vault over the horse?	¿ Puede usted saltar el burro a la garrocha ?
I can turn a somersault	Puedo dar el salto mortal
Can you recommend a teacher of Swedish gymnastics?	¿ Puede recomendarme un profesor de gimnasia sueca ?
The champion of the hundred-metre flat race is in good form this season	El campeón de los cien metros lisos está en plena forma esta temporada
For years now nobody has beaten the record of the one-thousand-metre relay race	Hace años que no se bate la marca de los mil metros por relevos
The school has a large gymnasium with all kinds of gymnastic apparatus	La escuela tiene un gimnasio grande con toda clase de aparatos de gimnasia

FOOTBALL
Vocabulary

FÚTBOL
Vocabulario

The match	El partido
The team	El equipo
The goalkeeper	El portero
The (right, left) back	El defensa (derecho, izquierdo)
The (right, left, centre) half-back	El medio (derecho, izquierdo, centro)
The forward line	La línea delantera
The inside (outside) right, left and centre forward	El interior (extremo) derecho, izquierdo y delantero centro

The home team	El equipo de casa
The away team	El equipo de afuera
The League	La Liga
The Division	La División
The semi-final	La semi-final
The final	La final
The Cup	La Copa
The referee	El árbitro
The goal	El gol, la portería
The cross-bar	El larguero
The goal-posts	Los postes
The net	La red
The score board	El marcador
The ball	El balón
The football pools	Las quinielas
The classification	La clasificación
The leader	El equipo en cabeza
To shoot	Chutar
To kick	Dar patadas
To kick off	Hacer el saque
To dribble	Regatear
To pass	Pasar
To score (goals)	Marcar (goles)
To mark	Marcar (al contrario)
To be on top	Dominar
To draw	Empatar
To win	Ganar
To beat	Derrotar, vencer
To lose	Perder

Phrases / Frases

Shall we go to the Valencia–Barcelona football match next Sunday afternoon?	¿ Quiere que vayamos al partido Valencia–Barcelona el próximo domingo por la tarde ?
Are they famous teams?	¿ Son equipos de categoría ?
The players wear boots and striped shirts	Los jugadores llevan botas y camisas a rayas

What a terrific shot!	¡ Vaya tiro más fenomenal !
Everybody is cheering	Todo el mundo anima a los jugadores
The public does not agree with the referee	El público no está conforme con el árbitro
The goal is well defended	La portería está bien defendida
The home team has already scored two goals	El equipo de casa ya ha marcado dos goles
What was the score?	¿ Cuál fué el tanteo ?
The right back is playing well	El defensa derecho las está dando todas
It was a wonderful goal	Ha sido un gol de bandera
They rounded off the attack with a good finish	Redondearon el ataque con un buen remate
Barcelona won three–two	Ganó el Barcelona por tres a dos
Does your team play in the next Cup-tie?	¿ Juega su equipo en la próxima eliminatoria de Copa ?
What is the capacity of the Madrid football ground?	¿ Cuál es la capacidad del campo de fútbol de Madrid ?
How many teams belong to the First Division?	¿ Cuántos equipos forman la Primera División ?

HOCKEY AND ICE-HOCKEY
Vocabulary

HOCKEY Y HOCKEY SOBRE HIELO
Vocabulario

The hockey stick	El palo del hockey
The ball (in hockey)	La pelota (en hockey)
The puck (in ice-hockey)	La pelota (en hockey sobre hielo)
The shin pads	Las espinilleras
The skates	Los patines
The ground or field	El campo de hockey
The ice rink	La pista de hielo
The side-lines	Las líneas laterales
The striking circle	El círculo de portería
The goals	Las porterías
The half-way line	La línea de medio campo

The teams	Los equipos
The goal-keeper	El portero
The backs	Los zagueros
The half-backs	Los medios
The forwards	Los delanteros
The bully	El golpe de salida
The corner	El saque de esquina
The penalty bully	El penalty-bully
The free hit	El golpe franco
The scoop stroke	El golpe de cuchara (elevando la pelota)
To roll-in	Poner la pelota en juego rodando
To strike, hit	Dar a la pelota

Phrases / Frases

Don't kick the ball	No le dé con el pie a la pelota
May I pick up the ball?	¿ Puedo coger la pelota del suelo ?
That's a foul	Es falta
At half-time our team was leading	En el primer tiempo iban por delante los nuestros
How many goals did they score?	¿ Cuántos tantos marcaron ellos ?
Did Madrid beat Tarrasa?	¿ Derrotó el Madrid al Tarrasa ?
Why is the umpire blowing his whistle now?	¿ Por qué toca el árbitro el silbato ahora ?
To indicate that the ball has passed wholly over the side-line	Para señalar que la pelota ha salido por fuera de la línea lateral
The hockey ball is very hard	La pelota de hockey es durísima
It is made of cork and string, and covered with white leather	Está hecha de corcho y bramante y recubierta de cuero blanco
The puck is made of rubber	La pelota para hockey sobre hielo es de goma

The rules allow you to bind the stick	El reglamento permite colocar vendajes en el palo
That player tackled on the left side, and the umpire blows his whistle for a foul	Aquel jugador hizo la entrada por la izquierda y el árbitro señala falta
Hockey is mostly an amateur sport	El hockey es mayormente un deporte de aficionados
There will be some hockey matches on roller skates during the forthcoming Olympic Games	En los próximos Juegos Olímpicos habrá varios partidos de hockey en patines de ruedas
This is an international ice-hockey match	Este es un partido internacional de hockey sobre hielo
The rules of this sport do not allow any unnecessary roughness	El reglamento de este deporte no permite ninguna rudeza innecesaria

LAWN TENNIS

Vocabulary

TENIS

Vocabulario

The tennis match	La partida de tenis
The tennis court	La cancha de tenis
The game	El juego
The set	El set
The singles match	La partida individual
The doubles match	La partida doble
The mixed doubles	La partida mixta
The racket	La raqueta
The tennis ball	La pelota de tenis
The net	La red
The base-line	La línea de base
The service-line	La línea del servicio
The server	El que sirve
The receiver	El que recibe
The umpire	El árbitro
The linesman	El linier
The cut	El corte

The smash	El smash
The lob	Voleo alto y tendido
The cannon (ball)	La pelota con efecto
Forehand	Derecho
Backhand	Revés
The volley	La volea
The rebound	El rebote
To serve	Sacar, servir
To spin	Girar la pelota
To take	Recoger, recibir
To return	Devolver
To be seeded	Ser seleccionado

Phrases	Frases
Do you play tennis?	¿ Juega usted al tenis ?
I am not a good player	No soy buen(a) jugador(a)
Are there any courts in the neighbourhood?	¿ Hay alguna cancha por aquí cerca ?
You can join our tennis club, if you like	Si lo desea, puede hacerse miembro de nuestra sociedad
Is the annual subscription very high?	¿ Es muy cara la subscripción anual ?
Have you brought your racket with you?	¿ Se ha traído la raqueta ?
I need new tennis shoes and half a dozen balls	Necesito unas zapatillas nuevas de tenis y media docena de pelotas
Throw this ball away, it does not bounce any more	Tira esa pelota, no bota ya
I must have my racket re-strung	Tengo que mandar a tensar la raqueta
Let us start with a singles and later we can fix some doubles with the club members	Empezaremos por una (partida) individual y luego arreglaremos alguna (partida) de dobles con miembros del club
Your service !	¡ Su servicio !
That was a fault ! Fault !	¡ Falta !

The umpire decided this ball was out	El árbitro decidió que la pelota había salido fuera
The ball touched the net	La pelota tocó la red
You must not take the ball on the volley	No debe recoger la pelota a la volea
Take the ball on the bounce	Recoja la pelota al rebote
Fifteen—thirty—forty—advantage all—advantage in (out)—Game	Quince — treinta — cuarenta—ventaja de los dos—ventaja del saque (del que recibe)—Juego
We had to play a set of eight to six	Tuvimos que jugar un set de ocho-seis
Have you seen a Wimbledon match?	¿ Ha visto usted alguna partida en Wimbledon ?
He is a seeded player	Es jugador de tenis seleccionado
How many are seeded ?	¿ Cuántos han sido seleccionados ?
Eight	Ocho
Are you a professional player ?	¿ Es usted jugador profesional ?
No, I play for fun	No; juego por entretenerme

GOLF   GOLF

Vocabulary   Vocabulario

The links, course	El campo de golf
The club house	El edificio de la sociedad
The professional's shop	La tienda especializada
The fairways	Los recorridos (hasta el césped)
The green	El césped (en torno al hoyo)
The hole	El hoyo
The hazards	Los obstáculos
The bunker	El talud
The rough	El campo abierto
The golf ball	La pelota de golf
The tee	La té
The club	El palo
The driver	El palo para tiro largo
The spoon	El palo de cabeza cóncava

The brassie	El palo de cabeza de latón
The mashie	El palo de cabeza ligeramente curva
The putter, etc.	El palo de cabeza recta, etc.
The golf bag	El saco de golf
The flag	La banderita
The stroke, drive	La jugada
The caddie	El cadi
To approach	Aproximarse
To putt	Afinar
To drive	Tirar largo la pelota

Phrases	Frases
Where is the nearest golf course?	¿ Dónde está el campo de golf más próximo ?
Are you a member of the local golf club?	¿ Es usted miembro del club de golf de esta ciudad ?
Is your friend a professional golfer?	¿ Es su amigo jugador profesional de golf ?
No, he is an amateur	No, es aficionado
Shall we play a whole round?	¿ Quiere usted que juguemos una ronda completa ?
What is your handicap?	¿ Qué ventaja necesita usted ?
You may tee up a second time	Puede colocar otra vez la pelota en la té
You have a good swing	Su balanceo es bueno
Use the driver for this stroke	Use usted el palo de tiro largo para esta jugada
You need another club for this chip shot, take number 5	Necesita otro palo para esta jugada en terreno difícil ; coja el número cinco
Play the ball from a hazard	Dele a la pelota desde el obstáculo
Let's play a foursome match	Vamos a jugar una partida de cuatro
What is the par (bogey) on these links?	¿ Cuál es el mínimo de jugadas en este campo de golf ?

It is a long way from the first tee to the last putting-green here	Hay un trecho largo desde la té del principio hasta el césped final
Do you carry all your thirteen different clubs?	¿ Trae usted los trece palos diferentes ?
He holed out on the sixteenth green	Metió la pelota de una jugada en el césped dieciséis
The woman amateur champion sank her ball like a professional	La campeona de aficionadas metió la pelota como un profesional
He missed too many shots in yesterday's threesome match	Ayer falló demasiadas jugadas en la partida de tres
Try not to falter on the fairways !	¡ Trate de no fallar en los recorridos !
The penalty for breach of this rule is loss of a hole	Se castiga con la pérdida de un hoyo al que no obedezca esta regla
Has the caddie found the ball which went astray?	¿ Encontró el cadi la pelota que se salió ?
No, he did not, I must send him to the shop to get some new ones	No la encontró ; tengo que enviarle a la tienda por unas pelotas nuevas
Are you competing in the International Golf Championship?	¿ Toma usted parte en el Campeonato Internacional de Golf ?

RIDING AND RACING

Vocabulary

LA MONTA Y LAS CARRERAS DE CABALLOS

Vocabulario

The riding horse	El caballo de montar
The racer	El caballo de carreras
The thoroughbred	El caballo de pura sangre
The stallion	El garañón
The mare	La yegua
The foal	El potro
The bay	El (caballo) bayo

The dapple grey	El (caballo) tordo
The white horse	El caballo blanco
The black horse	El caballo negro
The chestnut	El (caballo) alazán
The rider	El jinete, la amazona
The jockey	El jockey
The stud-owner	El dueño de la yeguada
The stable-owner	El dueño de la cuadra
The riding breeches	El pantalón de montar
The reins	Las riendas
The stirrup	El estribo
The spurs	Las espuelas
The saddle	La silla
The saddle girth	La cincha
The riding-school	La escuela de equitación
The turf	El césped
The race-course, track	El hipódromo
The groom	El palafrenero
The trot(ting)	El trote
The gallop(ing)	El galope
The canter(ing)	El galope corto
The flat-race	La carrera en liso
The steeplechase	La carrera de obstáculos
The hurdle-race	La carrera de vallas
The trotting-race	La carrera al trote
The winning post	La meta
The totalisator	El marcador
The winner	El vencedor
The betting	Las apuestas
The front legs	Las manos
The hind legs	Las patas
High School riding	Alta Escuela
The horse-shoe	La herradura
To ride	Montar (a caballo), cabalgar
To mount	Montar (en el caballo)
To dismount	Desmontar (del caballo)
To kick	Cocear

To buck	Arrojar al jinete por las orejas
To shy	Asustarse, caracolear
To bolt	Desbocarse
To back a horse	Apostar por un caballo
To neigh	Relinchar
To stamp	Piafar
By a length	Por un largo
Astride	A horcajadas
Side-saddle	A mujeriegas

Phrases	Frases
Is there a riding-school in this town?	¿ Hay alguna escuela de equitación en esta ciudad ?
I should like to hire a horse	Me gustaría alquilar un caballo
I need some riding-lessons	Necesito tomar lecciones de equitación
A course of riding-lessons costs a lot of money	Una serie de lecciones de equitación cuesta un dineral
Where can I hire a riding-outfit?	¿ Dónde podría alquilar un equipo de jinete ?
Have you any breeches?	¿ Tiene usted pantalones de montar ?
Where is my whip?	¿ Dónde está mi fusta ?
The horse is vicious	El caballo está resabiado
The mare is lame	La yegua está coja
Please harness the chestnut for me	Haga el favor de enjaezarme el alazán
Do you like to go to horse-races?	¿ Le gusta ir a las carreras de caballos ?
Where is the entrance to the race-course?	¿ Por dónde se entra al hipódromo ?
The nearest I was to a win was when I backed a placed horse	Lo más cerca que estuve de un premio fué cuando aposté por un colocado
My horse was scratched just before the start	Eliminaron mi caballo poco antes de empezar la carrera

There goes the jockey who won most races last year	Allí va el jockey que ganó más carreras la temporada pasada
Can you give me a good tip?	¿ Me puede dar un buen pronóstico ?
I have a hunch the French horse will win	Tengo el presentimiento de que el caballo francés va a ganar
To which stable does the winner belong?	¿ A qué cuadra pertenece el vencedor ?
Did you back the favourite?	¿ Apostó por el favorito ?
Where is the totalisator?	¿ Dónde está el marcador ?
The Madrid race-course is called La Zarzuela	El hipódromo de Madrid se llama La Zarzuela

HUNTING AND SHOOTING

LA CAZA Y EL TIRO

Vocabulary

Vocabulario

The huntsman, hunter	El cazador
The hounds, pack	Los sabuesos, la jauría
The meet	La partida de caza
The big-game hunt	La caza mayor
The bird shooting	La caza menor
The fox	El zorro
The wild boar	El jabalí
The mountain goat	La cabra montés
The fallow deer	El corzo
The stag	El ciervo, el venado
The rabbit	El conejo
The hare	La liebre
The game	La caza
The partridge	La perdiz
The pheasant	El faisán
The grouse	La perdiz blanca
The greyhound	El lebrel
The setter	El perro perdiguero
The pointer	El perro pachón
The hunting horn	El cuerno de caza
The bag	El zurrón

The rifle	El rifle
The gun	La escopeta
The butt	La culata
The barrel	El cañón
The trigger	El gatillo
The shot	La perdigonada
The sight	La mira
The cartridge	El cartucho
The snare	El lazo
The trap	La trampa
The hunting grounds	El coto
The target shooting	El tiro al blanco
The falling-plate shoot	El tiro al plato
To shoot	Disparar
To hit	Hacer blanco
To miss	Errar el tiro
To stalk	Acosar
To hunt	Cazar

Phrases / Frases

Is there any chance of hunting hereabouts?	¿ Hay probabilidades de que se cace algo por aquí ?
Would you care to go shooting hares with me?	¿ Le importaría venir a cazar liebres conmigo ?
My father has a shoot	Mi padre tiene un coto de caza
Is the hunting season for deer open?	¿ Han levantado la veda para la caza del ciervo ?
Did you bring home a good bag?	¿ Trajo para casa una buena zurronada ?
A brace of partridges and two rabbits	Una pareja de perdices y dos conejos
Are you a good shot?	¿ Tira usted bien ?
I have practised target shooting	He practicado al blanco
Did you clean your gun?	¿ Limpió usted su escopeta ?
Have your ever shot big game?	¿ Ha practicado usted alguna vez la caza mayor ?

I have been shooting in the Pyrenees	He tomado parte en una partida de caza en los Pirineos
Where can I buy a rifle?	¿Dónde puedo adquirir un rifle?
Can you let me have some cartridges?	¿Puede proporcionarme cartuchos?
What time in the morning did they call the hunters?	¿A qué hora de la mañana citaron a los cazadores?
The horns sounded at 6 a.m.	Tocaron los cuernos a las seis de la mañana
Were there many horses and hounds at the meet?	¿Había muchos caballos y sabuesos en la partida de caza?
There are still bears and eagles in some Spanish mountains	Todavía hay osos y águilas en algunas montañas de España

FISHING / LA PESCA

Vocabulary / Vocabulario

The fisherman	El pescador
The fishing-boat	El barco pesquero
The fishing-fleet	La flotilla pesquera
The fishing-tackle	Los avíos de pescar
The net	La red
The harpoon	El arpón
The angler	El pescador de caña
The fishing-rod	La caña de pescar
The fishing-line	El aparejo
The float, the bob	El corcho
The fish-hook	El anzuelo
The bait	El cebo
The worm	El gusano
The fly	La mosca
The salt-water fish	El pescado de mar
The herring	El arenque
The cod	El bacalao
The haddock	El pejepalo

The hake	La merluza
The halibut	El hipogloso
The turbot	El rodaballo
The sole	El lenguado
The whiting	La pescadilla
The tunny fish	El atún
The sardine	La sardina
The red mullet	El salmonete
The shell-fish	El marisco
The octopus	El pulpo
The crab	El cangrejo
The prawn	La gamba
The lobster	La langosta
The fresh-water fish	El pescado de agua dulce
The salmon	El salmón
The trout	La trucha
The carp	La carpa
The pike	El sollo
The eel	La anguila
The fish-bone	La espina
The fish-scale	La escama
The sea	El mar
The lake	El lago
The river	El río
The stream	El arroyo
The fish-pond	El vivero
To fish	Pescar
To angle	Pescar con caña
To bite	Picar

Phrases	Frases
Do you like fishing?	¿ Le gusta pescar ?
Do I need a licence to fish here?	¿ Necesito permiso para pescar aquí ?
Where can I buy fishing-tackle?	¿ Dónde puedo comprar avíos de pescar ?

I have forgotten to bring my fishing-rod	Me he olvidado de traer la caña de pescar
The bait is no good	El cebo no vale nada
Have you had a good catch?	¿ Ha cogido mucho ?
The fish are biting quickly to-day	Los peces pican bien hoy
Can one go out with the fishing-fleet?	¿ Se puede salir con la flotilla pesquera ?
What bait do you use for salmon-fishing?	¿ Qué cebo pone usted para pescar salmón ?
Is angling popular in Spain?	¿ Hay afición a la pesca de caña en España
Have you fried the fish we caught this morning?	¿ Ha frito usted el pescado que cogimos esta mañana ?
Is there a great variety of shell-fish on the Spanish coast?	¿ Hay mucha variedad de mariscos en las costas de España ?

SWIMMING

Vocabulary

LA NATACIÓN

Vocabulario

The bathing-resort	El balneario
The swimming-pool	La piscina
The bathing-costume	El traje de baño
The (swimming)-trunks	El calzón de baño
The bath-towel	La toalla de baño
The bathing-cap	El gorro de baño
The cabin	La cabina, la caseta
The attendant	El bañero
The lifebelt	El salvavidas
The artificial respiration	La respiración artificial
The cramp	El calambre
The diving-board	La palanca
The spring-board	El trampolín
The swimmer	El nadador, la nadadora
The breast stroke	Braza
The back stroke	Espalda
The butterfly stroke	Mariposa

The swallow dive	El salto del ángel
The beach	La playa
The sun-bathing	El baño de sol
The waves	Las olas
The shower	La ducha
To swim	Nadar
To dive	Bucear
To plunge	Zambullirse
To crawl	Nadar al crol
To shiver	Tiritar
To dry	Secar(se)
To float	Hacer la plancha
To drown	Ahogarse
To bathe	Bañarse

Phrases	Frases
Shall we have a swim (bathe)?	¿ Vamos a nadar ? (¿ Vamos a bañarnos ?)
Can we bathe in the river?	¿ Se puede bañar uno en el río ?
No, you must go to the swimming-pool	No, tiene usted que ir a la piscina
No bathing!	¡ Prohibido bañarse !
Are you a good swimmer?	¿ Es usted buen nadador ?
Let's swim to the opposite bank	Vamos a nadar hasta la otra orilla
The current is very strong	La corriente es muy fuerte
Can you swim on your back?	¿ Sabe usted nadar de espalda ?
He is floating	Está haciendo la plancha
Can you do the crawl?	¿ Sabe nadar al crol ?
I have got cramp in my left calf	Me ha dado un calambre en la pantorrilla izquierda
Swim and help him, he has gone under	Vaya nadando a ayudarle ; se ha sumergido
He was nearly drowned	Casi se había ahogado
Stay in the shallow water	Quédese donde cubra poco
Hang on to the life-line	Agárrese a la maroma

Don't swim beyond the danger sign	No nade más allá de la señal de peligro
This part of the swimming-pool is only for swimmers	Esta parte de la piscina es sólo para nadadores
Is there a vacant bathing-hut?	¿ Hay alguna caseta vacía ?
Can you recommend a pleasant seaside-resort?	¿ Podría recomendarme un sitio de veraneo agradable ?
The yellow flag means there is no undertow	La bandera amarilla indica que no hay resaca
Did you take part in the swimming championships?	¿ Tomó usted parte en el campeonato de natación ?
Who won yesterday's water-polo match?	¿ Quién venció ayer en el partido de polo acuático ?
There is an open-air swimming-pool in this town	En esta ciudad hay una piscina al aire libre

ROWING, BOATING
Vocabulary

EL REMO, LAS REGATAS
Vocabulario

The launch	La lancha
The boat	La barca, el bote
The rowing boat	La barca de remos
The punt	La lancha con pértiga
The yawl	La yola
The canoe	La canoa
The pirogue	La piragua
The collapsible boat	El bote plegable
The motor-boat	La (barca) motora
The skiff	La patinadora
The oar	El remo
The paddle	La paleta
The rudder	El timón
The sliding seat	El asiento corredizo
The oarsman	El remero
The cox	El timonel
The stroke	El golpe de remo
The crew	La dotación

The planks	El tablaje
The starboard	Estribor
The port	Babor
To row	Remar
To steer	Gobernar
To punt	Empujar con pértiga
To paddle	Remar con paleta
To float	Flotar

Phrases	Frases
Boats for hire	Se alquilan botes
Come to the jetty	Vengan al embarcadero
You can hire a boat on the pond in this park for five pesetas an hour	Se pueden alquilar botes en el estanque de este parque a cinco pesetas la hora
There is a strong head wind	Hay viento fuerte de proa
The boat leaks	La lancha hace agua
Let's go and watch the boat-race	Vámonos a ver la carrera de botes
Our Club won by two lengths	Nuestro equipo venció por dos largos
Are you a member of the Rowing Club?	¿ Es usted socio del Club Náutico ?
I should like to join your club	Quisiera hacerme socio de su club
I would like to see the San Sebastian race	Me gustaría presenciar las regatas de traineras de San Sebastián
I bought a small collapsible paddle-boat	He comprado un pequeño bote plegable

SAILING

Vocabulary

NAVEGACIÓN DE VELA

Vocabulario

The sailing boat	El balandro
The yacht	El yate
The sail	La vela
The mast	El mástil

The boom	El botalón
The keel	La quilla
The flag	La bandera
The lighthouse	El faro
The barge	La gabarra
The buoy	La boya
The anchor	El ancla
The breeze	La brisa
The dead calm	La calma chicha
The yachting season	La temporada de yates
The regatta	La regata de balandros
The course	El rumbo
To sail	Navegar
To strike	Arriar
To manœuvre	Maniobrar
To cruise	Efectuar un crucero
To reef	Arrizar
To drift	Ir a la deriva
To put into harbour	Arribar
To reach port	Llegar a puerto

Phrases

Frases

The sailing boat is anchored in the harbour	El balandro está anclado en el puerto
There is a fresh breeze to-day ; it is good sailing weather	Hace una brisa fresca hoy ; es buen tiempo para la vela
Weigh the anchor	Leven (el) ancla
Help me hoist the sails	Ayúdenme a izar las velas
Let's spend the day on the water	Vamos a pasar el día en el agua
Have you enough to eat with you ?	¿ Lleva usted bastante comida ?
Do you know anything about sailing ?	¿ Sabe usted algo de la navegación de vela ?
We have often cruised in the Mediterranean	Hemos efectuado frecuentes cruceros por el Mediterráneo
Is this yacht seaworthy ?	¿ Es marinero este yate ?

We were overtaken by the storm	Nos cogió el temporal
The boat is heeling over	El barco se está ladeando
The yacht has capsized	El yate ha zozobrado
There is a regatta out at sea this afternoon	Esta tarde hay una regata en alta mar
Set the course north, we have drifted too far westwards	Pon rumbo al Norte, hemos derivado demasiado hacia el Oeste

BOXING

Vocabulary

EL BOXEO

Vocabulario

The boxing match	El combate de boxeo
The wrestling match	El combate de lucha
The boxer	El boxeador
The wrestler	El luchador
The referee	El árbitro
The champion	El campeón
The feather-weight	El peso pluma
The fly-weight	El peso mosca
The light-weight	El peso ligero
The bantam-weight	El peso gallo
The cruiser-weight	El peso semipesado
The middle-weight	El peso medio
The welter-weight	El peso welter
The heavy-weight	El peso pesado
The trainer	El masajista
The coach	El entrenador
The seconds	Los '' segundos ''
The punch	El puñetazo
The round	El asalto
The ring	El cuadrilátero
The canvas	La lona
The ropes	Las cuerdas
The bell	El gong
The gloves	Los guantes

The towel	La toalla
The bandage	El vendaje
To box	Boxear
To wrestle	Luchar
To knock out	Noquear
To disqualify	Descalificar
To attack	Acometer
To cover up	Cubrirse
To take it	Encajar
To skip	Saltar a la comba
K.O.	Fuera de combate
On points	Por puntos
Technical knock-out	Fuera de combate técnico

Phrases

Frases

Would you care to see the match for the heavy-weight championship?	¿ Tendría interés en presenciar el combate para el título de peso pesado ?
The former world champion was knocked out in the sixth round	El que defendía el título de campeón mundial fué noqueado en el sexto asalto
Did he hit his opponent below the belt?	¿ Le dió golpe bajo al adversario ?
He floored him with a fierce upper-cut	Le derribó de un directo terrible
He was counted out in the third round	Le derribaron por más de la cuenta en el tercer asalto
The bell saved him from being knocked out	La campana le salvó del fuera de combate
He was pushed against the ropes, and his seconds threw in the towel	Le arrinconaron contra las cuerdas y sus '' segundos '' arrojaron la esponja
The boxers are skipping in the gymnasium to strengthen their legs	Los boxeadores saltan a la comba en el gimnasio para fortalecer las piernas
Is there a fight on to-night?	¿ Hay algún combate para esta noche ?

The two champions are competing	Luchan dos campeones
Did Romero defend his title?	¿ Defendió Romero su título ?
Are you an amateur boxer?	¿ Es usted boxeador aficionado ?

WINTER SPORTS	DEPORTES DE INVIERNO
Vocabulary	Vocabulario
The skis	Los esquís
The sticks	Los bastones, los palos
The wax	La cera
The skiing outfit	El equipo de esquiar
The skier	El esquiador, la esquiadora
The skiing jump	El trampolín de saltos
The ski-master, instructor	El profesor de esquí
The sledge	El trineo
The runners	Las cuchillas
The snow-plough	La apisonadora para nieve
The new snow	La nieve reciente
The snow-drift	La ventisca
The snowstorm	La tempestad de nieve
The powder snow	La nieve polvo
The ice	El hielo
The avalanche	El alud, la avalancha
The skates	Los patines de cuchilla
The skating-boots	Las botas de patinar
The skater	El patinador, la patinadora
The skating-rink	La pista de patinaje
The ice-show	La representación sobre hielo
To ski	Esquiar
To skate	Patinar
To jump	Saltar
To herring-bone up	Subir en tijera
To zig-zag up	Subir en zig-zag
To side-step up	Subir en escalera
To dance on ice	Bailar sobre el hielo
To freeze	Helar

Phrases	Frases
Can we hire skis here?	¿ Podemos alquilar aquí esquís ?
Is there a skiing instructor in this winter-resort hotel?	¿ Hay algún profesor de esquí en este parador de invierno ?
You can ask there on the spot; they will give you all kinds of information	Puede usted preguntar allí mismo ; le darán toda clase de información
Have your ever done any skiing?	¿ Ha esquiado usted antes ?
This new snow is not good for skiing	Esta nieve reciente no es buena para esquiar
Where can I buy a pair of skis and ski-sticks?	¿ Dónde podría comprar un par de esquís y bastones ?
Have you practised any stem-turns?	¿ Ha practicado virajes apoyados ?
I tried to learn to " Christy "	Intenté aprender la Cristianía
I'll take part in the slalom competition	Tomaré parte en la prueba de habilidad
Could you show me the way to the ski-jump?	¿ Me podría indicar cómo se va al trampolín ?
Don't forget to wax your skis	No se olvide de encerar sus esquís
I must adjust my bindings	Tengo que ajustarme las ataduras
Is there any bob-sleighing in Spain?	¿ Practican el bobsleigh en España ?
There are neither bob-runs nor toboggan-runs	No hay ni pistas de bob ni de tobogán
You can hire a sledge for the children near that slope	Puede alquilar trineos para los chicos cerca de aquella pendiente
Shall we go up by the mountain railway?	¿ Quiere que subamos en funicular ?
I don't like the crust on the snow; it is dangerous	No me gusta la corteza de la nieve ; es peligrosa
Do you like ice-skating?	¿ Le gusta patinar sobre hielo ?

The lake has frozen overnight	El lago se ha helado durante la noche
Does the ice bear?	¿ Aguanta el hielo ?
Be careful, it may thaw if the warmer weather continues	Tenga cuidado, puede haber deshielo si sigue tan templado
Get your skates and meet me at the skating-rink	Coja los patines de cuchillas y espéreme en la pista de patinaje
My skates are not much good for the outside-edge	Mis patines no son buenos para las curvas
You have not fixed your skates on well	No se ha atado usted bien los patines
There is a performance of figure-skating by torchlight this evening	Esta noche hay una representación de patinaje artístico con luz de antorchas

MOUNTAINEERING

Vocabulary

MONTAÑISMO

Vocabulario

The mountain	La montaña, el monte
The high mountains	Las altas montañas
The mountain range	La cordillera
The ridge of mountains	La sierra
The summit	La cima, la cumbre
The height	La altura
The rock	La roca, la peña
The glacier	El glaciar
The moraine	La morrena
The chasm, deep cavern	La sima
The chimney	La chimenea
The abyss	El abismo
The precipice	El precipicio
The valley	El valle
The crevasse	La grieta
The loose rocks	El terreno suelto

The mountain stream	El torrente
The ravine	La torrentera
The ascent	La ascención, la subida
The descent	El descenso, la bajada
The spelæology	La espeleología
The spelæologist	El espeleólogo
The mountaineer	El montañero
The alpinist	El alpinista
The guide	El guía
The mountain map	El mapa orográfico
The ice-axe	El piolet
The rope	La cuerda
The rucksack	La mochila
The nailed boots	Las botas de clavos
The blizzard	La ventisca
To climb	Escalar, trepar
To halt	Hacer alto
To reach the peak	Llegar a la cumbre
Steep	Escarpado, empinado
Flat	Llano

Phrases	Frases
Is there a guide in the village?	¿ Hay algún guía en el pueblo ?
I should like to go up to the glacier to-morrow morning	Me gustaría escalar hasta el glaciar mañana por la mañana
You must have a proper outfit	Tiene que proveerse de un equipo adecuado
Nailed boots are essential	Son esenciales botas de clavos
Shall I need a rope and an ice-axe?	¿ Voy a necesitar una cuerda y un piolet ?
The ascent is very steep	El ascenso es muy empinado
You will need irons when climbing the chimney	Necesitará usted martillos de escalada para trepar por la chimenea
Beware of the crevasses	Cuidado con las grietas
We shall have to spend the night in a mountain hut	Tendremos que pasar la noche en alguna cabaña

We might lose our way in the blizzard	Podríamos extraviarnos en la ventisca
We have left the clouds beneath us	Las nubes han quedado por debajo de nosotros
Do you like mountaineering?	¿ Le gusta el alpinismo ?
You will become snow-blind if you don't use your goggles	Le va a cegar el reflejo de la nieve, si no se pone las gafas
Can you let me have some cream for sun-burn?	¿ Me puede dejar la crema contra la quemadura del sol ?
Can we get something to eat and drink at the mountain dairy farm?	¿ Podremos conseguir algo de comer y beber en la granja ?
They lost their way, and a rescue party set out to find them	Se extraviaron y un equipo de salvamiento salió a buscarles
The injured mountaineers were brought down on stretchers	Bajaron en camillas a los montañeros heridos
Did you have an easy climb yesterday?	¿ Tuvo usted una subida fácil ayer ?
We reached the summit at noon	Llegamos a la cumbre a medio día
What mountains are there in this region?	¿ Qué montes hay en esta región ?

PELOTA

Vocabulary

The " frontón ", (Pelota ground)	El frontón
The playing court	La cancha
The front wall	El frontis
The side-wall	El blé
The squares into which the side-wall is divided	Los cuadros
The lines marking the limit between " good " and " fault "	Los escases

PELOTA VASCA

Vocabulario

The teams	Los bandos
The Blues	Los Azules
The Reds	Los Rojos
The ball-boy	El intendente
The ball	La pelota
The bat	La pala
The curved basket	La cesta de punta
The bookmakers	Los corredores
The betting ticket	La traviesa
The pools	Las quinielas
The points	Los tantos
To play with the hands	Jugar a mano
To catch the ball with the curved basket and hit it back	Encestar
To serve	Sacar
To bounce	Rebotar
Good	Buena
Fault	Falta

Phrases	Frases
Are you coming with me to the Jai-Alai frontón?	¿Viene usted conmigo al frontón Jai-Alai?
One of to-day's matches promises to be interesting	Una de las partidas de hoy promete ser interesante
What kind of pelota are they playing: with the hand, with a bat, or with a basket?	Cómo es: ¿a mano, a pala o a cesta?
The scorer is shouting the score of the last game	El tanteador vocea los tantos del último juego
It seems they score as in tennis	Parece que el tanteo se hace como en el tenis
The ball should hit the wall above the white line and bounce behind the black line on the floor	La pelota tiene que rebotar en la pared por encima del escás blanco y en el suelo por detrás del escás negro

The player is now serving a cannon ball	Ese pelotari lanza ahora la pelota con efecto
The basket flings the ball off at an enormous speed as if flung from a sling	Con la cesta la pelota sale disparada como con honda a una velocidad enorme
They are tossing a coin to decide who may choose the ball from the ball-boy's bag	Están tirando a cara o cruz para ver quién escoge la pelota del saco del intendente
Pelota is very popular in Madrid, Barcelona and the towns and villages of Northern Spain	La pelota vasca es muy popular en Madrid, en Barcelona y en las ciudades y pueblos del Norte de España

INDOOR GAMES

Games of chance (*juegos de azar*) are played in family circles as well as in those public places which allow them. Twice a month there is a National Lottery (*Lotería Nacional*) with substantial prizes, while the famous traditional Christmas Draw (*Sorteo de Navidad*) has a first prize called the *premio gordo* worth fifteen million pesetas (about £140,000 under the present exchange rate).

In many cafés games of dice and billiards are played ; but card games are available only in *tabernas* (pubs).

In provincial towns and elsewhere you will find *casinos*, which are really clubs, where people meet to talk or to play all kinds of games.

Chess is played everywhere and, in addition to the annual national championship, there are local competitions of varying standards for people of all ages. (Chess is a popular game with teenagers in Spain.)

Card-playing enjoys popularity, especially among adults. Incidentally, the Spanish packs of cards have different designs from ours. *Oros* (or coins) are equivalent to our diamonds,

Copas (or cups) are like our hearts, *Espadas* (or swords) represent our spades and *Bastos* (sticks or clubs) our clubs. Instead of Queens you will find *Caballos* (horses), while the Jack or Knave is called a *Sota*.

Every card game is played, especially canasta. But apart from poker and bridge, which are played by only a minority, the games which are most popular and typically Spanish are *tute*, *mus* and the difficult *tresillo*, which have no counterpart in England.

INDOOR GAMES	JUEGOS
Vocabulary	Vocabulario
The draughts	Las damas
The draughtboard	El tablero de damas
The king	La dama
The " man ", piece	La pieza
The chess	El ajedrez
The chess-board	El tablero de ajedrez
The queen	La reina, la dama
The king	El rey
The knight	El caballo
The rook, castle	La torre
The bishop	El alfil
The pawn	El peón
The dice	Los dados
The dice-box	El cubilete
The roulette	La ruleta
The lottery	La lotería
The skittles	Los bolos
The billiards	El billar
The cannon	La carambola
The chalk	La tiza
The cue	El taco
The pocket	La tronera
The dominoes	El dominó
The pack of cards	El paquete de naipes, la baraja
The player	El jugador

The dummy	El que duerme
The suits	Los palos
Hearts	Oros
Diamonds	Copas
Spades	Espadas
Clubs	Bastos
The ace	El as
The king	El rey
The queen	El caballo
The jack, knave	La sota
The joker	El comodín
The trumps	Los triunfos
To play	Jugar
To gamble	Jugar por dinero
To take a piece	Comer una pieza
To castle the king	Enrocar
To check	Dar jaque
To checkmate	Dar mate
To cast dice	Tirar a los dados
To play cards	Jugar a las cartas
To shuffle	Barajar
To deal	Dar, repartir
To cut	Cortar
To declare	Cantar
To ruff	Fallar
To take a trick at cards	Hacer baza
To follow suit	Asistir al palo
To trump	Triunfar

Phrases	Frases
Do you often play at draughts?	¿ Juega usted con frecuencia a las damas ?
No, I am more interested in chess	No, me interesa más el ajedrez
It is your turn to move	Le toca jugar a usted
I castle the king	Me enroco

I wonder if I should exchange a knight and a bishop for that castle	No sé si cambiar caballo y alfil por esa torre
Whites to play	Juegan las blancas
If you move this pawn your queen is in danger	Si mueve ese peón deja al descubierto la dama
I challenge you to a game of table tennis	Les desafío a una partida de ping pong
He is good at playing snooker	Es buen jugador de billar inglés
Have you ever seen a pool game?	¿ Ha visto usted alguna vez una partida de billar americano ?
I will give you ten cannons	Le doy de ventaja diez carambolas
We can play at three cushions	Podemos jugar a tres bandas
Shall we play billiards or cards?	¿ Jugamos al billar o a las cartas ?
Have you a new pack?	Tiene usted baraja nueva ?
I have shuffled, you cut	He barajado ; corte
You deal	Su mano
Who will score?	¿ Quién va a apuntar ?
Whose call is it?	¿ Quién canta ?
I pass	Paso
Diamonds are trumps	Pintan copas
Your play, your turn	Juega usted
You must follow suit	Tiene usted que asistir al palo
This is my trick	Esta baza es mía
I must discard	Tengo que descartarme
Don't look at my cards	No me mire las cartas
Lay the cards on the table	Ponga las cartas sobre la mesa
I have lost 100 pesetas at cards	He perdido cien pesetas a las cartas
Gambling has been his ruin	Se ha arruinado con el juego
He has won the kitty	Se ha llevado el pote
He took over the bank	Se hizo cargo de la banca

F

BULLFIGHTING

In Spain, bullfighting is the national sport or entertainment. From March to October every local fair has its corresponding bullfight (*corrida*), while in the large cities there are *corridas* or *novilladas* (that is, bullfights with young bulls), every Thursday and Sunday.

In a programme there are usually three chief bullfighters (*espadas* or *matadores*) who fight and kill six bulls, but occasionally two rivals fight the six between them in what is known as a *mano a mano*.

The senior bullfighter takes on the first and then the fourth bull, the next man the second and the fifth, and the junior the third and the sixth or last, *que cierra plaza*. On a special occasion the senior *matador* will let the junior take the *alternativa*; that is, he recognises the junior as a *matador*, and allows him to fight and kill the first bull that afternoon, lending him his own sword (*estoque*) and acting, as it were, as a godfather. The other *matador* acts as a witness.

Before the actual fight begins, all the bullfighters and attendants parade wearing their colourful costumes and carrying their beautiful cloaks, and a horseman gallops to catch the key to the bull pen, thrown to him by the President from his box.

The three *matadores*, helped by the team (*cuadrilla*) of the one who is to kill the bull, play the animal with their cloaks for the first *tercio* (or third of the time allotted to each bull). In the second *tercio* the bull *toma las varas*; that is, it charges the *picadores*, who are mounted and carry pikes or lances to wound and gore the bull as it attacks. Next it receives three pairs of darts (*banderillas*), which are planted home by the *banderilleros* in the neck of the animal as it rushes towards them. For the third *tercio*, the matador takes his cloak and sword (*los trastos*) and fights the bull, playing it first with his cloak suspended from and controlled by a kind of stick (*muleta*), and then with his sword before he finally goes in to kill (*entra a matar*). The time allowed to each *matador* for despatching the bull is limited. If he takes longer than ten minutes he is warned by the

President, and if on the third warning (fifteen minutes) he has still not managed to kill the bull, he is in disgrace, and the bull is led out of the ring by a few cows.

The *matador* usually fights in honour of a friend, of some young lady or of the public in general. This is indicated when he *brinda el toro*. If he excels in his fight, he is sometimes given an ear from the bull as a souvenir.

After a bull is killed there is an interval for the removal of the carcase and for covering up the blood that remains. A bugle call announces the entrance of the next bull.

For centuries the art of bullfighting has been associated with Spanish life, and so it is not strange that bullfighting terms should colour the everyday language of the people, just as cricket does in English. For example,

> *A mi no me torea usted ;* You are not going to make fun of me.
>
> *Fuerte como un toro*, as strong as a bull.

Bullfighting is undoubtedly cruel, but attractive and, whatever people may say or think, foreign tourists flock to see a *corrida*, even if, after a time, they have to look from " behind cupped hands ".

THE BULLFIGHTING
Vocabulary

EL TOREO
Vocabulario

The art of fighting bulls	El toreo
The bullfight	La corrida de toros
The bullfight with bulls under three years old	La novillada
The bullfighter	El torero
The bullfighter who sticks *banderillas*	El banderillero
The small decorated dart	La banderilla
The mounted bullfighter	El picador
The matador	El matador, el espada
The matador on horse-back	El rejoneador
The bullfighter's team on foot	Los peones

The attendants	Los monosabios
The ring	El ruedo
The arena	La plaza de toros
(The section) in the shade	La sombra
(The section) in the sun	El sol
The first barrier	La barrera
The second barrier	La contrabarrera
The narrow path between the two barriers	El callejón
The rows of uncovered seats	El tendido
The seats of the amphitheatre (gallery)	La grada
The upper circle	La andanada
The gala cloak	El capote de paseo
The bullfighting cloak	El capote de torear
The hat	La montera
The trousers	La taleguilla
The bullfighter's costume	El traje de luces
The bull	El toro
The bull's pen	El toril
The under-three-years-old bull	El novillo
The horns	Los cuernos
The nape	El morrillo
The ear	La oreja
The tail	El rabo
The legs	Las patas
The breed-badge	La divisa (de la ganadería)
The gore	La cornada
The rapier or sword	El estoque
The thrusting of the rapier	La estocada
The performance	La faena
The breast pass	El pase de pecho
The change of manœuvre	El cambio de suertes
The ovation	La ovación
The applause	El aplauso
The hand clappings	Las palmas
The cheers	Los olés

The walk round the ring	La vuelta al ruedo
The drawing of lots	El sorteo
The bullfighting clutch	La muleta
Dragging the dead bull out of the arena is called—	El arrastre
To fight bulls	Torear
To stick in banderillas	Banderillear
To wound the bull (by the picador)	Picar
To kill the bull	Matar

Phrases	Frases
Shall we go to the bullfight this afternoon?	¿ Quiere que vayamos esta tarde a los toros ?
It all depends on the programme	Depende del cartel
It is a bullfight with picadores and bulls under three years old	Es una novillada de picadores
What is the breed of these bulls?	¿ De qué divisa son los toros ?
They come from an Andalusian breeder	Son de una ganadería andaluza
There are only uncovered seats in the sun; those in the shade are sold out	Sólo quedan tendidos de sol ; los de sombra están todos vendidos
At last Sunday's bullfight there were many women with Manila shawls and with carnations in their hair	En la corrida del domingo pasado había muchas mujeres con mantones de Manila y claveles en el pelo
Which is our *tendido*? (uncovered stand)	¿ Cuál es nuestro tendido ?
Number nine, so we shall be in the shade after the third bull	El nueve, así que después del tercer toro tendremos sombra
How many bulls will be fought?	¿ De cuántos toros es la corrida ?

Next Sunday there will be six, but Sunday week there will be eight

El domingo próximo será de seis, pero del domingo en ocho días será de ocho

The six bulls were cast by lots among the three bullfighters this morning

Esta mañana se sortearon los seis toros entre los tres matadores

The new matador will fight the third bull

Al matador nuevo le toca torear el tercer toro

Hurry up, the band is already playing the *pasodoble* (a lively march tune)

Dése prisa, que ya están tocando el pasodoble

Why are there fences to separate one part of the crowd from the other?

¿ Para qué son esas verjas que dividen la plaza en dos mitades ?

To prevent people with tickets for the sunny side climbing over to the section in the shade

Para evitar que el público de sol se pase al de sombra

The parade begins

Empieza el paseíllo

The bullfighter clad in pink and silver is an outstanding *novillero* (fighter of young bulls)

El torero que va vestido de rosa y plata es un novillero puntero

Must the cloaks always be red to make the bull charge?

¿ Tienen que ser siempre rojos los capotes para que embista el toro ?

No.　Bulls are colour-blind

No.　Los toros no distinguen los colores

Why does the bugle sound?

¿ Por qué tocan el clarín ?

Because the second *tercio* is about to begin

Es porque va a empezar el segundo tercio

What do you call the bullfighter who is approaching the bull without a cloak?

¿ Cómo se llama ese torero que se acerca al toro sin capote ?

He is the banderillero.　He will now stick in the first pair of darts (into the bull's neck)

Es el banderillero.　Va a poner el primer par de banderillas

Why does he run to the cover at the barrier?

¿ Por qué corre al burladero ?

He tries to hide from the bull, so as not to be caught by him

Quiere esconderse para que el toro no le coja

Could the picador's horse be gored?

¿ Puede coger el toro al caballo del picador ?

It is not likely, as the horse is protected by a strong lined cover

No es probable, porque el caballo va protegido por un peto

Why does the picador wound the bull with a lance?

¿ Por qué clava el picador a toro una vara ?

To sap the animal's strength

Para restar fuerzas al animal

Now a bullfighter is stepping forward with a red cloth

Ahora se adelanta un torero con una franela roja

It is the matador carrying a *muleta* in his left hand

Es el matador y lleva la muleta en la izquierda

He is very brave.   See what a close pass ! Bravo !

Es muy valiente. ¡ Fíjese qué pase tan ceñido ! ¡ Olé !

People stand up and wave their handkerchiefs

La gente se levanta agitando los pañuelos

They are requesting the president to grant the bullfighter the ear of the bull (as a prize)

Piden al presidente que conceda al matador la oreja del toro

And does he not want to?

¿ Y no quiere concedérsela ?

No, he does not, because the bullfighter has failed twice to kill the bull

No, porque el torero ha tenido que pinchar tres veces para matar al toro

The matador must aim at the nape of the bull with his rapier

El matador tiene que clavar el estoque en el morrillo

The senior bullfighter was allowed to walk round the arena after his first bull

Al torero más antiguo se le concedió dar la vuelta al ruedo en el primer toro

His performance was very courageous

Su faena fué muy valiente

Everybody is throwing his hat into the ring	Todo el mundo arroja el sombrero al ruedo
The matador and his team pick the hats up and return them to the audience	El espada y sus subalternos van recogiendo los sombreros y devolviéndoselos a los espectadores
Some people are throwing cigars, and a young lady has thrown one of her shoes, out of sheer enthusiasm	Hay quien tira puros y una señorita, de puro entusiasmo, ha tirado un zapato
Now, the attendants take the dead bull away, hauling him out tied to a carriage drawn by mules	Ahora los monosabios hacen el arrastre del toro con las mulillas
The matador will be carried out of the main gate on the shoulders of his admirers	El torero va a salir a hombros de los aficionados por la puerta grande

THE TIME

On the building of the *Ministerio de la Gobernación* in the *Puerta del Sol* in Madrid there is a clock whose chimes, like those of Big Ben in London, give the Spaniards the Official Time, which is based on the Meridian of Greenwich. English " summer-time ", however, is kept in Spain the whole year through.

If you ask a Spaniard to tell you the time, never forget to say *por favor* (please).

Spanish calendars have always black figures for the ordinary working days, whereas Sundays and special *días de fiesta* (public holidays), whether political or religious, are printed in red. But there are so many " red-letter " days, exclusive of Sundays, in the Spanish calendar that they equal or even exceed the number of Sundays. The days of the week are not necessarily spelt with an initial capital letter in Spanish.

Business hours are nine to one and three or four to seven, with modification in the summer when some offices work straight through from 8 a.m. to 2 p.m. This is called a *jornada intensiva*.

Breakfast is taken about eight, lunch at two, and supper at ten o'clock. These long intervals between meals are rather trying for English visitors in Spain.

It is not uncommon for Spanish people to go out after supper. Midnight is not considered too late an hour, and the streets are still alive with people at that time of night, especially in the summer.

THE TIME	EL TIEMPO
Vocabulary	Vocabulario
The watch	El reloj
The wrist-watch	El reloj de pulsera
The sundial	El reloj de sol
The clock	El reloj de pared
The church-bell	El reloj de torre
The alarm clock	El despertador
The hands	Las manecillas
The dial, the face	La esfera
The second-hand	El segundero
The minute-hand	El minutero
The hour-hand	El horario
The watchmaker	El relojero
The second	El segundo
The minute	El minuto
The hour	La hora
The day	El día
Sunday	Domingo
Monday	Lunes
Tuesday	Martes
Wednesday	Miércoles
Thursday	Jueves
Friday	Viernes
Saturday	Sábado

The week	La semana
The month	El mes
January	Enero
February	Febrero
March	Marzo
April	Abril
May	Mayo
June	Junio
July	Julio
August	Agosto
September	Setiembre
October	Octubre
November	Noviembre
December	Diciembre
The seasons	Las estaciones
The spring	La primavera
The summer	El verano
The autumn	El otoño
The winter	El invierno
The year	El año
The leap year	El año bisiesto
The century	El siglo
The working-days	Los días de trabajo, laborables
The public holiday	El día de fiesta
The holidays	Las vacaciones
Christmas	Navidad
Easter	Pascua
Whitsun	Pentecostés
The morning	La mañana
The noon, midday	El medio día
The afternoon	La tarde
The evening	La tarde, la noche
The night	La noche
The midnight	La media noche
The moon	La luna
The star	La estrella
The sun	El sol

The calendar	El calendario
The sunrise	El amanecer, la aurora
The sunset	El atardecer, el ocaso
The eclipse	El eclipse
The full moon	La luna llena
The new moon	La luna nueva
The first quarter	El cuarto creciente
The third quarter	El cuarto menguante
The modern age	La edad moderna
The Middle Ages	La edad media
In olden times	En los tiempos antiguos
The present	El presente
The past	El pasado
The future	El futuro
Summer-time	Horario de verano
The twilight	El crepúsculo
Early	Temprano
Late	Tarde
Punctual	Puntual
In good time	A tiempo
In advance	Con antelación, con anticipación
To wind up	Dar cuerda
To repair	Arreglar
To get up	Levantarse
To go to bed	Acostarse
To get up early	Madrugar
To go to bed late	Trasnochar

Phrases	Frases
Can you tell me the right time ?	¿ Podría decirme la hora exacta, por favor ?
Is your watch right ?	¿ Marcha bien su reloj ?
It is five minutes fast	Va cinco minutos adelantado
It is a quarter of an hour slow	Va atrasado un cuarto de hora
It always keeps good time	Marca siempre la hora justa
What time is it ?	¿ Qué hora es, me hace el favor ?

It is eight o'clock sharp	Son las ocho en punto
It is five minutes past eight	Son las ocho y cinco
It is a quarter-past eight	Son las ocho y cuarto
Half-past eight	Las ocho y media
A quarter to nine	Las nueve menos cuarto
One a.m.	La una de la madrugada
Eight a.m.	Las ocho de la mañana
Three p.m.	Las tres de la tarde
Eleven p.m.	Las once de la noche
It is noon	Es mediodía
The train leaves at 2.30	El tren sale a las dos treinta
You will have to be at the station half an hour beforehand	Tendrá usted que estar en la estación media hora antes
Don't be late	No llegue tarde
I shall be in time	Llegaré a tiempo
It is time to get up (to go to bed)	Es hora de levantarse (de acostarse)
Hurry up, it is half-past seven	Dése prisa, son las siete y media
My alarm clock has stopped	Se me ha parado el despertador
I must take my watch to the watchmaker	Tengo que llevar mi reloj al relojero
It needs cleaning	Necesita que lo limpien
The glass is cracked	Se ha rajado el cristal
Set your watch by the station clock	Ponga su reloj por el de la estación
Next month there will be a concert	El mes que viene habrá un concierto
I shall be back in a week	Volveré dentro de una semana
A fortnight ago I was in London	Hace quince días estaba en Londres
It gets dark very early	Oscurece muy pronto
What is the date to-day?	¿ A qué fecha estamos ?
To-day is the fifteenth of September	Hoy es el quince de setiembre
My birthday is on the tenth of October	Mi cumpleaños es el diez de octubre

Are you going away this year?	¿ Sale usted de viaje este año ?
I came back the day before yesterday	Regresé anteayer
I shall be leaving again to-morrow (the day after to-morrow, next week)	Me iré de nuevo mañana (pasado mañana, la semana que viene)
Don't arrive at the last minute	No llegue en el último minuto
One moment, please	Perdone un minuto
At dawn	Al amanecer
At dusk	Al oscurecer
Last year was a leap year	El año pasado fué bisiesto
Can you spare me a moment?	¿ Podría atenderme un momento ?
I have no time	No tengo tiempo
It is getting late	Se está haciendo tarde
Please call for me early	Venga a buscarme pronto, por favor
He left long ago	Se fué hace tiempo
This building is two centuries old	Este edificio tiene dos siglos
How old are you?	¿ Cuántos años tiene usted ?
I was thirty-six last January	Cumplí treinta y seis años en enero
This gentleman is middle-aged	Este señor es de media edad
This is an elderly lady	Es una señora mayor
This is an old lady	Es una señora vieja, de edad avanzada
He is older than his brother	Es mayor que su hermano
She is younger than her sister	Ella es más joven que su hermana

THE WEATHER

In spite of its situation in the South of Europe, Spain does not, as one might believe, enjoy a semi-tropical climate. The main reason for this lies in the mountainous structure of the terrain, which, in Europe, is second only to Switzerland in this respect. Three-quarters of the country form a vast tableland (*meseta*), whose average height is 2,700 feet above sea-level and which is crossed from East to West by several ranges of mountains. On the Southern and Eastern sides it slopes down gently towards the coast, but on the North the last buttresses of the Pyrenees shorten the length of the fall towards the coast, and so it is very abrupt.

The different zones caused by these irregularities give the Iberian peninsula a great variety of climates. While the West and North have moderate and rainy weather, with temperatures similar to those of South-west England, the tableland suffers from a rigorous Continental climate, with its long, cold, dry spells in winter and intense heat in summer. The South and East are blessed with a mild Mediterranean climate.

Notwithstanding, everything said about the sun in Spain is true. Even in winter it shines very brightly, although it is not hot. In summer it causes a dazzling glare on the dry Spanish plains.

The temperature is measured on the Centigrade scale, and varies between 20° below zero (which is under 0° Fahrenheit) in Teruel during the winter and above 40° Centigrade (which is above 105° Fahrenheit) in Córdoba during the summer.

Although the wireless and the newspapers give daily forecasts, the weather is not a very usual topic of conversation among Spaniards. One is allowed to make some brief observation on it, but it is not considered to be very witty to draw out this topic of conversation for more than three minutes, unless the conversation takes place in the Meteorological Observatory !

THE WEATHER	EL TIEMPO (CLIMATOLÓGICO)
Vocabulary	**Vocabulario**
The climate	El clima
The weather	El tiempo
The air	El aire
The heat	El calor
The warmth	El calor moderado
The cold	El frío
The rain	La lluvia
The snow	La nieve
The sun(shine)	El sol
The thunderstorm	La tormenta
The thunder	El trueno
The lightning	El relámpago
The thunderbolt	El rayo
The hail	El granizo
The ice	El hielo
The thaw	El deshielo
The sky	El cielo
The cloud	La nube
The wind	El viento
The gale	El temporal
The tempest	La tempestad
The hurricane	El huracán
The breeze	La brisa
The fog	La niebla
The mist	La bruma
The dew	El rocío
The frost	La escarcha
The horizon	El horizonte
The rainbow	El arco iris
The cardinal points	Los puntos cardinales
North	Norte
East	Este
South	Sur

West	Oeste
The compass (card)	La rosa de los vientos
The tide	La marea
The ebb	El reflujo
The flow	El flujo
The sea, ocean	El (la) mar, el océano
The flood	La inundación
The atmosphere	La atmósfera
Fine weather	Buen tiempo
Bad weather	Mal tiempo
Cold	Frío
Chilly	Fresco
Warm, hot	Caluroso, caliente
Temperate, lukewarm	Templado
Hot	Muy caliente
It is freezing	Está helando
It is snowing	Está nevando
It is raining	Está lloviendo
The sun is coming out	Está saliendo el sol
The sun rises	Amanece, el sol se levanta
The sun sets	Oscurece, el sol se pone
The sky is overcast	El cielo está nublado

Phrases	Frases
What is the weather like?	¿ Qué tal tiempo hace ?
It is fine	Hace buen tiempo
It is a lovely day	Hace un día precioso
The weather is beautiful (dull)	El tiempo está espléndido (gris)
The weather is changeable	El tiempo está variable
The weather is settled	El tiempo está seguro
It is hot (cold)	Hace mucho calor (frío)
It is rainy	Está de lluvia
It is foggy	Está de niebla, hace niebla
It is very slippery, be careful	Está muy resbaladizo ; tenga cuidado
It's a nice evening !	¡ Qué noche más agradable hace !

It is very close, sultry	Está muy bochornoso
Do you think the weather will remain fine?	¿Cree usted que seguirá haciendo buen tiempo?
The North wind is cold	El viento del Norte es frío
It is stormy	Está de tormenta
The wind has dropped	El viento ha amainado
It is raining in torrents (cats and dogs)	Llueve a torrentes (a cántaros)
It is pouring	Está diluviando
I am wet through	Estoy empapado/a
Where is my umbrella?	¿Dónde está mi paraguas?
Take a mack(intosh), raincoat	Llévese el impermeable
Will there be a thunderstorm?	¿Habrá tormenta?
It's lightening and thundering	Hay relámpagos y truenos
The sky is completely overcast	El cielo está completamente cubierto
The sky is clear	El cielo está despejado
It is clearing up	Está despejando
It's too sunny here, let's sit in the shade	Hace demasiado sol aquí; nos sentaremos a la sombra
It is getting chilly	Está poniéndose fresco
Are you cold?	¿Tiene frío?
I feel hot	Tengo mucho calor
It is warm in here	Hace calor aquí dentro
I can't stand the heat	No aguanto el calor
It's a warm day	Es un día caluroso
It is a warm climate	Es un clima cálido
How many degrees is it by the thermometer?	¿Cuántos grados marca el termómetro?
It has gone up to 22° (Centigrade)	Ha subido a veintidós grados (centígrados)
The glass is rising (falling)	El barómetro sube (baja)
The meteorological station is high up on that hill	La estación meteorológica está en lo alto de esa colina
They broadcast the weather report every day	Todos los días se radia el boletín meteorológico
The atmosphere is clear	La atmósfera está limpia

SOCIAL LIFE

Nearly all civilised countries have more or less the same standards of social behaviour. Nevertheless, there are differences of expression if not of standards. For example, when you visit a Spaniard in his home, he says to you as you leave, " You have taken possession of your home " (*Ha tomado usted posesión de su casa*) or, " You know now where your home is " (*Ya sabe usted donde tiene su casa*). But this is a mere formality based on the assumption that you will not take advantage of it to go and occupy his best room !

Similarly, expressions such as " At your feet, madam " (*A sus pies, señora*) do not have to be taken literally. They are merely phrases, like the English " terribly sorry ", which imply that they will not be believed at their face value, although to omit them would be considered rude.

When guests rise to depart the hostess will say, " Must you go ? " (*¿ Qué prisa tienen ?*) ; yet, not to say this could be interpreted as a sign of relief.

Nobody should enter or leave a place where others are eating without saying, *¡ Qué aproveche !* (like the French *bon appétit*) to which the answer will be, *¿ Usted gusta ?* (" Won't you join us ? "). Social etiquette demands a refusal with the words, *Muchísimas gracias* (" Many thanks ") whether they are sincere or not.

In introductions after, *Le presento al señor Artime* (" May I introduce Mr. Artime ? "), you reply *Muchísimo gusto* (" With much pleasure "), to which the answer will be, *Encantado* (" charmed "). On leaving, he will say, *Celebro haberle conocido* (" Delighted to have met you ").

Because it is a country where they have not fought for their rights, Spanish women have to suffer constantly the *tortura de la galantería* (" the torture of compliments and attention "). Although men do not always now get up to offer ladies a seat in the bus or the underground, they still use the *piropo* in all places—that is, they pass remarks, complimentary or otherwise, as the lady goes by (something like the G.I.'s " whistling a

dame "). Strangely enough, Spanish women seem to put up with this state of affairs.

When it is hard to decide whether it is evening or night, the correct thing in Spanish is to say, *Buenas tardes* (" good evening ") while daylight lasts, and *Buenas noches* (" good night ") after twilight.

When people leave off work the usual thing to say is, *Hasta mañana* (" See you to-morrow ") rather than " Good night ".

THE SOCIAL LIFE	LA VIDA DE RELACIÓN
Vocabulary	**Vocabulario**
The visit, call	La visita
The invitation	La invitación
The party	La fiesta, la reunión
The appointment	La cita
The meeting	La entrevista
The talk, chat	La charla
The reception	La recepción
The visiting-card	La tarjeta de visita
The acquaintances	Los conocidos
The (close) friends	Los amigos (íntimos)
The neighbours	Los vecinos
To invite	Invitar
To visit, to call on	Visitar
To ring the bell	Llamar al timbre
To arrive	Llegar
To be punctual	Ser puntual
To be late	Llegar tarde
To welcome	Dar la bienvenida
To take leave	Despedirse
To expect, to wait for	Esperar, esperar a
To meet (a friend in the street)	Encontrar (a un amigo en la (calle)
To have to meet (a friend)	Tener que ver (a un amigo)
Meet (my friend John)	Permítame que le presente (a mi amigo Juan)

To introduce	Presentar
To say good-bye	Decir adiós
To make an appointment (with)	Citarse (con)
To make conversation, to converse	Trabar conversación, conversar

Phrases

PAYING A CALL

Frases

DE VISITA

Did you ring the bell?	¿ Fué usted quien llamó al timbre ?
Is Mrs. García at home ?	¿ Está la señora García en casa ?
Please come in	Tenga la bondad de pasar
Mrs. López wishes to speak to you	La señora López desea hablar con usted
Show the visitor in	Haga pasar a la visita
Very pleased to see you	Encantado/a de verle/a por aquí
It is a great pleasure to me	Tengo sumo gusto
The pleasure is mine	El gusto es mío
Thank you for your kind invitation	Muchas gracias por su amable invitación
It was very kind of you to invite me	Ha sido usted sumamente amable al invitarme
Make yourself at home	Está usted en su casa
You are very kind	Es usted muy amable
My parents send their kind regards	Mis padres le envían recuerdos
Am I late (early)?	¿ Llego tarde (pronto) ?
May I introduce my husband ?	¿ Me permite que le presente mi marido ?
Here are my son and my daughter	Aquí están mi hijo y mi hija
Please sit down	Tenga la bondad de sentarse
Have some tea and cake ?	¿ Un poco de tarta con el té ?
Please help yourself	Sírvase usted mismo/a
Do stay to dinner (supper)	Quédese a comer (cenar)

Next time you must stay with us	La próxima vez tendrá que quedarse con nosotros
Can you put me up for to-night?	¿ Podría usted acomodarme esta noche ?
I am sorry but I must go	Lo siento, pero no tengo más remedio que irme
Do stay a little longer	Quédese un ratito más
I must not miss my train	No debo perder el tren
I hope you'll come again soon	Confío que volverá pronto
Come whenever you like	Ya sabe donde tiene su casa
Many thanks for your hospitality	Muchas gracias por su hospitalidad
Could we meet for lunch to-morrow ?	¿ Podríamos encontrarnos mañana para comer juntos ?
Sorry, I have a prior engagement	Lo siento ; tengo ya un compromiso
I have nothing on the day after to-morrow	Pasado mañana estoy completamente libre

GREETINGS

SALUDOS

Good morning ; good day	Buenos días
Good evening ; good night	Buenas tardes ; buenas noches
How are you?	¿ Qué tal le va ? ¿ Cómo está usted ?
Delighted	Encantado/a
Pleased to see you	Encantado/a de verle
Haven't seen you for a long time	Hace mucho que no le/a veía
What a pleasant surprise to see you !	¡ Qué agradable sorpresa el verle/a !
We must keep in touch with each other	Tenemos que seguir viéndonos
Good-bye ; see you again soon	Adiós ; a ver si nos vemos pronto
Pleasant journey	Feliz viaje
Good luck. All the best	Buena suerte. Que todo salga bien

Keep well	Usted siga bien
Cheerio	Que le vaya bien
Cheers !	¡ Salud !
Don't forget us	No se olvide de nosotros

REQUESTS

PETICIONES, ENCARGOS

A cup of coffee, please	Una taza de café
May I trouble you for a match (a light)?	¿ Haría el favor de darme una cerilla (lumbre) ?
May I ask you to do me a favour?	¿ Puedo pedirle un favor ?
Would you be good enough to post this letter for me?	¿ Tendría la bondad de echarme esta carta ?
I have a request to make	Quisiera encargarle una cosa
I don't want to be disturbed	No quiero que me molesten
She asks for help	(Ella) está pidiendo socorro
I wish I were already at home	Desearía estar ya en casa
Would you assist me?	¿ Podría usted ayudarme ?
Your request will be granted	Su petición será concedida
Have you applied for your passport?	¿ Ha solicitado usted su pasaporte ?
May I open the window?	¿ Puedo abrir la ventana ?
Do you mind if I close the door?	¿ Le importa que cierre la puerta ?
May I apply for the job?	¿ Puedo solicitar este empleo ?
I should like to hear your opinion	Me gustaría saber qué opina usted
What do you want?	¿ Qué desea ?
Can I help you?	¿ Puedo servirle en algo ?
Don't bother	No se moleste

THANKS

GRACIAS

Thank you ; thanks	Muchas gracias ; gracias
Many thanks	Muchísimas gràcias
I am very grateful to you	Le estoy muy agradecido/a

I am very much obliged to you	Le quedo muy obligado/a
I am deeply indebted to you	Le quedo infinitamente reconocido/a
You are very kind (good)	Es usted muy amable (bueno/a)
You have done me a great favour	Me ha prestado usted un gran favor
I wish I could repay you	Quisiera poder corresponder
Please accept my sincere thanks	Le ruego acepte mi agradecimiento más sincero
I should like to thank you for the present	Quisiera darle las gracias por el regalo

REGRETS, APOLOGIES

DISCULPAS, EXCUSAS

I am sorry you are ill	Siento que esté usted enfermo/a
I am sorry for you	Lo siento por usted
I regret the misunderstanding	Lamento este malentendido
May I express my regrets?	¿ Puedo expresarle mi sentimiento ?
It is very regrettable	Es muy de lamentar
Let me express my condolences	Permítame que le dé el pésame
Pardon. Sorry	Perdón. Lo siento
I beg your pardon	Usted perdone
Please forgive me	Le ruego me perdone
I did not want to hurt your feelings	No quise herir sus sentimientos
It was not my fault	No fué culpa mía
I did not do it on purpose	No lo hice a propósito (Lo hice sin querer)
Don't be angry	No se enfade
Please don't take offence	No lo tome a mal, se lo ruego
Don't think me impolite (rude)	No me crea descortés (mal educado)
Please put it down to my ignorance	Acháquemelo a ignorancia

ENQUIRIES

Where is the station?

Can you direct me to the post-office?

Is this the way to the theatre?

Is there a bus-stop near here?

Where is the booking-office?

Where can I change money?

Where can I leave my luggage?

Can you get me a taxi?

Which is the best hotel of this town?

Can I have a room for one night?

Where is the lift?

Are there any letters for me?

Where does Mr. Rivero live?

Does Mr. Iglesias live here?

Has anybody called?

Was there any telephone message for me?

Could you inform me of . . . ?

PREGUNTAS

¿ Dónde está la estación?

¿ Podría encaminarme a la Casa de Correos?

¿ Voy bien por aquí para el teatro?

¿ Hay por aquí cerca alguna parada de autobús?

¿ Dónde está la taquilla?

¿ Dónde podría cambiar dinero?

¿ Dónde podría dejar mi equipaje?

¿ Podría buscarme un taxi?

¿ Cuál es el mejor hotel en esta ciudad?

¿ Podría tomar una habitación por una noche sólo?

¿ Dónde está el ascensor?

¿ Hay alguna carta para mí?

¿ Dónde vive el señor Rivero?

¿ Vive aquí el señor Iglesias?

¿ Ha llamado alguien?

¿ Ha habido algún recado por teléfono para mí?

¿ Podría informarme sobre si . . . ?

PUBLIC NOTICES

Caution!

Look out!

Mind the step (gap)

Do not touch, highly dangerous

Danger. High-tension current

Private property. No admittance

AVISOS PÚBLICOS

¡ Cuidado!

¡ Atención!

Cuidado con el peldaño (la zanja)

No tocar; peligro de muerte

Peligro. Corriente de alta tensión

Propiedad privada. Prohibido el paso

Keep off the grass	Prohibido caminar sobre el césped
Trespassers will be prosecuted	Prohibido el paso a toda persona ajena a este recinto
Wet paint	Recién pintado
Stick no bills	Prohibido fijar carteles
Beware of the dog	Cuidado con el perro
Beware of pickpockets	Cuidado con los rateros
No hawkers	No se permite traficar
You may telephone (from) here	Teléfono público
Entrance; way in	Entrada
Emergency exit	Salida para casos de peligro
Exit; way out	Salida
Push	Empuje, empujad
Pull	Tire, tirad
Vacant	Libre
Engaged	Ocupado
Road up	Carretera en reparación
Keep to the right (left)	Vaya por la derecha (izquierda)
Drive slowly	Despacio
Diversion	Desviación
No thoroughfare	Paso interceptado
One-way street	Dirección única
Main road ahead	Carretera principal
No traffic	Circulación prohibida
Crossing for pedestrians	Cruce para peatones
No parking	Prohibido aparcar
Red	Rojo
Amber	Amarillo
Green	Verde
No smoking	Prohibido fumar
Private	Privado
Closed	Cerrado
Do not lean out of the window	Prohibido asomarse al exterior

BOOKS, NEWSPAPERS

When you read a Spanish newspaper you are struck by the large amount of space given to news from abroad compared with that devoted to home news.   Most of the big dailies have their own correspondents in places like London, Paris, New York, Buenos Aires, because Spaniards are always curious to know what goes on in the outside world.

Lately, as a result of Spain's strategic position on international air routes, many famous personalities land or stay in Spain, and Spanish newspapermen have adopted the modern fashion of interviewing V.I.P.'s.

Most Spanish towns boast a Public Library, and excellent taste is shown in the editing and publishing of books.   There are a number of moderately priced editions on India paper (*papel biblia*) bound in good leather.   Every Spring in Madrid there is an Exhibition of Books which is well worth a visit.

As would be expected in a country with such a reputation and tradition in art, there are plenty of good artists in Spain and some of their excellent work is reflected in the magazines, and in illustrated books for children and grown-ups.

BOOKS, NEWSPAPERS	LIBROS, PERIÓDICOS
Vocabulary	Vocabulario
The bookshop	La librería
The public library	La biblioteca pública
The volume	El volumen, el tomo
The edition	La edición
The binding	La encuadernación
The guide-book	La guía
The novel	La novela
The bookstall	El kiosco de periódicos
The press	La prensa
The newspaper	El periódico
The daily	El diario
The weekly	El semanario

The monthly	La publicación mensual
The illustrated paper	El periódico ilustrado
The technical (professional) journal	La revista técnica (profesional)
The trade journal	La revista comercial
The official bulletin	El boletín oficial
The comic	El tebeo
The fashion magazine	La revista de modas
The review	La revista
The leader	El artículo de fondo
The news	Las noticias
The short story	La novela corta
The column	La columna
The cartoon	El chiste gráfico
The review (book, film, theatre)	La crítica (de libros, cine, teatro)
The headlines	Los titulares
The advertisement	El anuncio
The publisher	El editor
The editor	El redactor
The journalist	El periodista
The reader	El lector
The printer	El impresor
The print	La impresión
The bookseller	El librero
The newspaper vendor	El vendedor de periódicos
To publish	Publicar
To print	Imprimir
To read	Leer
To skim through	Hojear
Out of print	Agotado

Phrases	Frases
Have you any edition of the Spanish classics?	¿ Tiene ediciones de los clásicos españoles ?
Have you any modern literature?	¿ Tiene libros de literatura moderna ?

Can you recommend a good guide-book?	¿ Podría recomendarme una buena guía ?
I want the edition of the Complete Works of Calderón in four volumes	Desearía la edición de las Obras Completas de Calderón en cuatro tomos
Please show me some illustrated books on Spanish painting (sculpture)	Tenga la bondad de enseñarme algún libro con láminas sobre pintura (escultura) española
Haven't you a bound copy of this novel?	¿ No tiene ningún ejemplar encuadernado de esta novela?
I want a good Spanish–English pocket dictionary	Quisiera un buen diccionario de bolsillo Español–Inglés
Have you a lending library?	¿ Tiene biblioteca circulante ?
Please bring me the morning paper	Tráigame el periódico de la mañana
Has the evening paper come out?	¿ Ha salido ya el periódico de la noche ?
Are these the latest periodicals on economic matters?	¿ Son estas las últimas publicaciones sobre cuestiones de economía ?
Have you read the leader?	¿ Ha leído usted el artículo de fondo ?
What's the news?	¿ Qué noticias hay ?
The latest news is on the right hand column of the front page	Las noticias de última hora se encuentran en la columna de la derecha de la primera página
Please let me have a weekly paper	Hágame el favor de un semanario
Let me have a comic paper, please	Hágame el favor de un tebeo
Do you stock English papers?	¿ Tiene periódicos ingleses ?
Could you lend me your paper for a minute?	¿ Podría prestarme su periódico un segundo ?
Have you read the advertisements ?	¿ Ha leído usted los anuncios ?

I have read the section " Situations Vacant " (" Situations Wanted ")	He leído la sección de " Ofrecen empleo " (" Buscan empleo ")
Which is the best fashion magazine?	¿ Cuál es la mejor revista de modas ?
Have you a map of Madrid?	¿ Tiene usted el plano de Madrid ?
The bookstall at the corner has them	Se vende en el puesto de periódicos de la esquina
Do you subscribe to a daily paper?	¿ Está usted subscrito/a a algún diario ?
I have applied for a yearly subscription of this magazine	He solicitado una subscripción anual de esta revista
Do you read the national and international press?	¿ Lee usted la prensa nacional y la extranjera ?

THE HOUSE

In Spanish towns most people live in flats. The caretaker (*portero/a*) or concierge, is responsible for collecting and distributing mail, cleaning the stairs and entrance hall, answering enquiries and so on.

The cellar, or that part of the building below ground level, is called the *sótano*, and is rarely used as living-quarters. From the ground floor (*piso bajo*) upwards the flats are numbered first (*primero*), second, third, etc. : although in some buildings the first is called the *entresuelo* (abbreviated to *entlo.*), the second, the *principal* (abbreviated to *pral.*), and the third then becomes the *primero*, and the fourth the *segundo* and so on.

The climate differs in different parts of the country and so, in the North, the houses have slanting roofs made of tiles or slate, but in Castilla and the South the roofs are usually flat. This flat roof, called a terrace (*terraza*), is for the common use of the tenants who use it for sun-bathing as well as drying

clothes. In buildings where there is a slanting roof, the top floor is called the *guardilla*; where the roof is flat, the *ático*.

Each floor usually has two *pisos* (flats), left and right (*izda.* and *dcha.* when abbreviated) : but in some big buildings you will also find centre (*centro*) and even centre right (*centro derecha*) and centre left (*centro izquierda*). Sometimes, however, the flats are simply lettered A, B, C, D, E, etc. Those flats with balconies overlooking the street are called *exteriores*, and those with windows looking on to a courtyard are called *interiores*.

The balcony windows and ordinary windows have shutters as a rule, and open like French windows.

Normally there is ample central heating—if not, the Spaniards use the traditional *mesa camilla*. This is a round table covered by a large table-cloth. Underneath the table is placed the famous *brasero* (a charcoal fire in a large covered dish made of bronze). The family sit around this table, with their legs and sometimes arms and hands under the table for warmth.

Domestic servants are still fairly easy to find ; but they must be addressed as *usted* until you know them very well. The maids do not like to be referred to as *criadas* : the usual word for a maid is *muchacha* or *chica*. She, in her turn, refers to her master and mistress as the *señorito* or *señorita*, although they may be married.

THE HOUSE	LA CASA (LA VIVIENDA)
Vocabulary	Vocabulario
The building	El edificio
The flat	El piso, el apartamento
The storey	El piso, la planta
The cellar	El sótano
The ground floor	La planta baja
The attic	La guardilla, el ático
The roof	El tejado, la terraza
The wall	La pared, el tabique
The window	La ventana
The balcony	El balcón

The glass-covered balcony	El mirador
The door	La puerta
The key	La llave
The room	La habitación, el cuarto
The floor	El suelo, el piso
The ceiling	El techo
The drawing-room	El cuarto de estar
The dining-room	El comedor
The study	El gabinete de trabajo, el despacho
The bedroom	La alcoba, el dormitorio
The dressing-room	El tocador
The nursery	El cuarto de los niños
The hall	El vestíbulo
The bathroom	El cuarto de baño
The bath-(tub)	La bañera, el baño
The wash-basin	El lavabo
The lavatory	El inodoro
The stairs	La escalera
The banisters	El pasamanos
The furniture	Los muebles
The stove	La estufa
The central-heating	La calefacción central
The radiator	El radiador
The curtain	La cortina
The blind	La persiana
The shutter	La contraventana
The brazier	El brasero
The switch	La llave de la luz
The lamp	La lámpara
The carpet	La alfombra
The table	La mesa
The chair	La silla
The easy-chair	El sillón
The mirror	El espejo
The sideboard	El trinchero
The cupboard	El armario

The bed	La cama
The couch	El diván
The bedside table	La mesilla de noche
The pillow	La almohada
The blanket	La manta
The sheet	La sábana
The eiderdown	El edredón
The bedspread	La colcha
The kitchen	La cocina
The kitchen range	La batería de cocina
The gas (electric) cooker	La cocinilla de gas (eléctrica)
The coal fire	La lumbre de carbón
The pan	La cazuela, la olla
The saucepan	La cacerola
The frying-pan	La sartén
The cutlery	Los cubiertos
The crockery	La vajilla, la loza
The tea-pot	La tetera
The coffee-pot	La cafetera
The gas (electric, water) meter	El contador del gas (de la electricidad, del agua)
The pantry	La despensa
To cook	Guisar, cocinar
To live	Vivir, habitar
To move in (out)	Mudarse a(de)
To lease	Arrendar
To rent	Alquilar

Phrases

Frases

Rooms to let	Se alquilan habitaciones
Have you taken a furnished flat?	¿ Ha alquilado usted un piso amueblado ?
I want a furnished room with the use of the kitchen	Desearía una habitación amueblada con derecho a cocina
I want to buy a house with garden	Quiero comprar una casa con jardín
Where do you live?	¿ Dónde vive usted ?

I live on the second floor, to the right	Vivo en el segundo piso a mano derecha
I live on the top floor	Vivo en la guardilla (en el ático)
The staircase has fresh paint	La escalera está recién pintada
Is your friend upstairs?	¿ Está su amigo arriba ?
He is downstairs in the dining-room	Está abajo, en el comedor
I want an airy and spacious room	Quiero una habitación ventilada y espaciosa
I am looking for a bed-sitting-room	Estoy buscando un cuarto para todo
This room looks on to the park	Esta habitación da al parque
This building has many storeys and four flats on each floor	Este edificio tiene muchos pisos de cuatro viviendas cada uno
I need a writing desk and book-cases	Necesito una mesa de escritorio y estanterías para libros
Is the bed comfortable?	¿ Es cómoda la cama ?
It is too hard (too soft)	Es muy dura (muy blanda)
Switch the light on (off)	Encienda (Apague)
Save light!	¡ No malgaste la luz !
The lamp on the bedside table has no bulb	La lámpara de la mesilla de noche no tiene bombilla
Can I have a bath?	¿ Puedo tomar un baño ?
There is no hot water to-day	Hoy no hay agua caliente
Where is the maid?	¿ Dónde está la muchacha ?
The chambermaid and the cook are in the kitchen	La doncella y la cocinera están en la cocina
The table is laid for lunch in the dining-room	La mesa para el almuerzo ha sido servida en el comedor
The knives, forks, teaspoons and tablespoons are in the sideboard-drawer	Los cuchillos, los tenedores, las cucharillas y las cucharas están en el cajón del aparador
This crockery is chinaware	Esta vajilla es de porcelana
The plates, saucers, cups and dishes are kept locked up	Los platos, los platillos, las tazas y las fuentes han sido puestos bajo llave

G

This flat has central-heating	Este piso tiene calefacción central
Our old cottage has only braziers	Nuestra vieja casa de campo tiene sólo braseros
Bring another chair to this corner of the drawing-room	Traiga otra silla a este rincón del cuarto de estar
This door needs a new lock	Esta puerta necesita una cerradura nueva
The latch-key is lost	Se ha extraviado el llavín
There is an iron bolt on the front door	La puerta de la casa tiene un cerrojo de hierro
What is the monthly rent for this flat ?	¿ Qué renta al mes este piso ?
Must I pay in advance ?	¿ Tengo que pagar por adelantado ?
Could I move in next month ?	¿ Podría ocuparlo el mes que viene ?
When did you move out of your old flat ?	¿ Cuándo se mudó usted de la casa anterior ?
Are you the owner of this house ?	¿ Es usted el propietario de esta casa ?
I have only a lease for one year	Sólo la he arrendado por un año

COUNTRIES AND NATIONS

In Spanish, adjectives and nouns of nationality are never introduced with a capital letter as in English. Names of countries usually are used without the article, as in English, but the following exceptions should be noted : *la* Argentina, *el* Brasil, *el* Ecuador, *la* India, *el* Japón, *el* Paraguay, *el* Uruguay ; but, of course, Francia, Italia, Inglaterra, España, etc.

América or *americano* do not, as do the English words America and American, apply generally to North America or even the U.S.A. The Spaniards use these words to denote the whole of

the " New World " (*Nuevo Mundo*) and all its inhabitants. Nor does the Spaniard refer to the countries of Latin America, but rather to the Spanish-speaking countries of America (*los países americanos de habla española*). North America is called *Norteamérica* or *América del Norte*. South America, similarly, is either *Sudamérica* or *América del Sur*.

Spain is divided into fifty provinces grouped under fifteen regions. National unity was not achieved until the fifteenth century in the reign of the Catholic Monarchs (Ferdinand and Isabella), and the fact that throughout the Middle Ages the Peninsula remained cut up into independent kingdoms has meant that the customs and the speech of the people of one region often differ from those of a neighbouring one and even sometimes from town to town.

To form an adjective from a geographical name (e.g., of a town or province, etc.) one adds a suffix such as ANO/A, EÑO/A, ENSE, ÉS/A, etc. Thus from Valencia one gets *valenciANO/A*; from Cáceres, *cacerEÑO/A*; from Lérida, *leridENSE*; from Alava, *alavÉS/A*.

Occasionally for phonetic and other reasons the adjective has a different look; e.g., from Cuenca one gets *conquense*; from Burgos, *burgalés/a*; from Madrid, *madrileño/a*; from Galicia, *gallego/a*.

Sometimes there is no apparent connection; e.g., from Calatayud the adjective *bilbilitano/a* is formed; the reason is that the original Roman name of this town was *Bilbilis*.

COUNTRIES AND NATIONS	PAÍSES Y NACIONES
Vocabulary	Vocabulario
Africa	África
The African, African	africano/a
Albania	Albania
The Albanian, Albanian	albano/a
America	América
The American, American	americano/a
Arabian	Arabia

The Arabian, Arabian	árabe
Argentine	(República) **Argentina**
The Argentinian, Argentinian	argentino/a
Asia	Asia
The Asiatic, Asiatic	asiático/a
Australia	Australia
The Australian, Australian	australiano/a
Austria	Austria
The Austrian, Austrian	austríaco/a
Belgium	Bélgica
The Belgian, Belgian	belga
Brazil	Brasil
The Brazilian, Brazilian	brasileño/a
Bulgaria	Bulgaria
The Bulgarian, Bulgarian	búlgaro/a
Canada	Canadá
The Canadian, Canadian	canadiense
Chile	Chile
The Chilean, Chilean	chileno/a
China	China
The Chinese, Chinese	chino/a
Czecho-Slovakia	Checoeslovaquia
The Czech(o-Slovak), Czechic	checo(eslovaco/a)/a
Denmark	Dinamarca
The Dane, Danish	danés/a
Egypt	Egipto
The Egyptian, Egyptian	egipcio/a
England	Inglaterra
The Englishman/woman, English	inglés/a
Europe	Europa
The European, European	europeo/a
Finland	Finlandia
The Finn, Finnish	finlandés/a
France	Francia
The Frenchman/woman, French	francés/a

Germany	Alemania
The German, German	alemán/a
Great Britain	Gran Bretaña
The Britisher (Briton), British	británico/a
Greece	Grecia
The Greek	griego/a
Holland	Holanda
The Dutchman/woman, Dutch	holandés/a
Hungary	Hungría
The Hungarian, Hungarian	húngaro/a
India	India
The Indian, Indian	indio/a
Ireland	Irlanda
The Irishman/woman, Irish	irlandés/a
Italy	Italia
The Italian, Italian	italiano/a
Japan	Japón
The Japanese, Japanese	japonés/a
Jugoslavia	Yugoeslavia
The Jugoslav, Jugoslav	yugoeslavo/a
Luxemburg	Luxemburgo
The Luxemburger, Luxemburger	luxemburgués/a
Mexico	México
The Mexican, Mexican	mexicano/a
New Zealand	Nueva Zelanda
The New Zealander, New Zealand	neozelandés/a
Norway	Noruega
The Norwegian, Norwegian	noruego/a
Persia	Persia
The Persian, Persian	persa
Poland	Polonia
The Pole, Polish	polaco/a
Portugal	Portugal
The Portuguese, Portuguese	portugués/a
Roumania	Rumanía
The Roumanian, Roumanian	rumano/a
Russia	Rusia

The Russian, Russian	ruso/a
Scotland	Escocia
The Scotsman/woman, Scottish	escocés/a
Spain	España
The Spaniard, Spanish	español/a
Sweden	Suecia
The Swede, Swedish	sueco/a
Switzerland	Suiza
The Swiss, Swiss	suizo/a
Turkey	Turquía
The Turk, Turkish	turco/a
The United States of America (U.S.A.)	Los Estados Unidos de América (EE.UU.)
The North American, North American	norteamericano/a
Wales	Gales
The Welshman/woman, Welsh	galés/a

REGIONS, ISLANDS, TOWNS	REGIONES, ISLAS, CIUDADES
Alexandria	Alejandría
Algiers	Argel
Antwerp	Amberes
Athens	Atenas
Balearic Isles	Islas Baleares
Bâle	Basilea
Bavaria	Baviera
Bethlehem	Belén
Bilboa	Bilbao
Biscay	Vizcaya
Bordeaux	Burdeos
Bruges	Brujas
Brussels	Bruselas
Burgundy	Borgoña
Canary Islands	Islas Canarias

Ceylon	Ceilán
Corsica	Córcega
Cyprus	Chipre
Dunkirk	Dunquerque
Edinburgh	Edimburgo
Flandres	Flandes
Genoa	Génova
Geneva	Ginebra
Greenland	Groenlandia
Hague	La Haya
Havana	La Habana
Iceland	Islandia
Jerusalem	Jerusalén
Lapland	Laponia
London	Londres
Marseilles	Marsella
Mediterranean	Mediterráneo
Morocco	Marruecos
Naples	Nápoles
Netherlands	Países Bajos
Newfoundland	Terranova
New York	Nueva York
Nice	Niza
Philippine Islands	Islas Filipinas
Pyrenees	Pirineos
Rome	Roma
Saragossa	Zaragoza
Sardinia	Cerdeña
Saxony	Sajonia
Scandinavia	Escandinavia
Thames	Támesis
Tangier	Tánger
Tunis	Túnez
United Kingdom	Reino Unido
Venice	Venecia
Vienna	Viena
Warsaw	Varsovia

REGIONS AND PROVINCES OF SPAIN	REGIONES Y PROVINCIAS ESPAÑOLAS
Andalusia	Andalucía
Andalusian	andaluz/a
	Almería—almeriense
	Cádiz—gaditano/a
	Córdoba—cordobés/a
	Granada—granadino/a
	Huelva—onubense
	Jaén—jaenés/a
	Málaga—malagueño/a
	Sevilla—sevillano/a
Aragon	Aragón
Aragonese	aragonés/a
	Huesca—oscense
	Teruel—turolense
	Zaragoza—zaragozano/a
Asturias	Asturias
Asturian	asturiano/a
Balearic Islands	Islas Baleares
Balearic	balear
	Mallorca—mallorquino/a
Basque Provinces	Provincias Vascongadas
Basque	vasco/a
	Álava—alavés/a
	Guipúzcoa—guipuzcoano/a
	Vizcaya—vizcaíno/a
Canary Islands	Islas Canarias
Canarian	canario/a
Catalonia	Cataluña
Catalan	catalán/a
	Barcelona—barcelonés/a
	Gerona—gerundense
	Lérida—leridano/a
	Tarragona—tarraconense
New Castile	Castilla la Nueva

Castilian	castellano/a
	Ciudad Real—ciudad-realeño/a
	Cuenca—conquense
	Guadalajara — guadalajareño/a
	Madrid—madrileño/a
	Toledo—toledano/a
Old Castile	Castilla la Vieja
Castilian	castellano/a
	Ávila—abulense
	Burgos—burgalés/a
	Logroño—logroñés/a
	Santander—santanderino/a
	Segovia—segoviano/a
	Soria—soriano/a
Estremadura	Extremadura
Estremenian	extremeño/a
	Badajoz—badajocense
	Cáceres—cacereño/a
Galicia	Galicia
Galician	gallego/a
	La Coruña—coruñés/a
	Lugo—lucense
	Orense—orensano/a
	Pontevedra—pontevedrés/a
Leon	León
Leonese	leonés/a
	León—leonés/a
	Palencia—palentino/a
	Salamanca—salmantino/a
	Valladolid—vallisoletano/a
	Zamora—zamorano/a
Murcia	Murcia
Murcian	murciano/a
	Albacete—albaceteño/a
	Murcia—murciano/a

Navarra	Navarra
Navarrese	navarro/a
Valencia	Valencia
Valencian	valenciano/a
	Alicante—alicantino/a
	Castellón de la Plana—caste-llonense
	Valencia—valenciano/a

Phrases	Frases
What is your nationality?	¿ Qué nacionalidad tiene usted ?
I am English (Spanish, French, German, South American)	Soy inglés (español, francés, alemán, sudamericano)
Have you any identification papers?	¿ Tiene usted algún documento de identidad ?
I have a British (Spanish, French, Italian) passport	Tengo pasaporte británico (español, francés, italiano)
How long have you been here?	¿ Cuánto hace que está usted aquí ?
Here is my identity card	Aquí tiene mi carnet de identidad
I am Spanish by birth	Soy español de nacimiento
I am English by marriage	Soy inglesa por matrimonio
From what country do you come?	¿ De qué país viene usted ?
I am stateless	Carezco de nacionalidad
Can I claim Spanish nationality?	¿ Puedo solicitar la nacionalidad española ?
Are you a naturalised Britisher?	¿ Se ha naturalizado británico ?
I want to travel to the Argentine	Quisiera ir a la Argentina
Can I enter Portugal without a special visa?	¿ Puedo entrar en Portugal sin visado especial ?
My mother tongue is Spanish	Mi lengua madre es el español
Are you a foreigner?	¿ Es usted extranjero/a ?

I have travelled through Spain	He viajado por España
He has returned from the Canary Islands	Ha regresado de las Islas Canarias
Are you a Mexican subject?	¿ Es usted súbdito mexicano ?
Do you speak English (Spanish, French, Portuguese)?	¿ Habla usted inglés (español, francés, portugués) ?
I can only speak a little Spanish	Hablo sólo un poco de español
I can read it, but I cannot speak it fluently	Puedo leerlo, pero no hablarlo de corrido
I shall have to take Spanish lessons	Tendré que tomar lecciones de castellano
Can you recommend a good native teacher?	¿ Puede recomendarme un buen profesor nativo ?
Can you understand me?	¿ Me entiende usted ?
You have an Andalusian accent	Tiene usted acento andaluz
Do you understand the Galician dialect?	¿ Entiende usted el dialecto gallego ?
Do you speak Catalan?	¿ Habla usted el catalán ?
I have studied the Basque language	He estudiado el vascuence
I did not understand you	No le entendí
I could not get your sentence	No me enteré de su frase
Please speak a little more slowly	Tenga la bondad de hablar un poco más despacio
Could you please translate this paragraph for me?	¿ Tendría la bondad de traducirme este párrafo ?
How do you spell this word?	¿ Cómo se escribe esta palabra ?
I'll spell it out for you	Se la voy a deletrear
You have a good (bad) pronunciation	Tiene usted buena (mala) pronunciación
Would you act as an interpreter for me with this gentleman?	¿ Querría servirme de intérprete para con este señor ?

ARMY, NAVY, AIR FORCE

Compulsory military service lasts two years in Spain, and begins at the age of twenty-two. Exemptions are granted to men who are unfit for various medical reasons, such as suffering from certain classes of illness or disease, or having lost an arm or a leg. A man is also given exemption if his father is over sixty years of age, or if he is the only son of a widow and can prove that he is the only supporter of the family.

At the beginning of January of the year in which the future recruit reaches the age of twenty-one, he is called up for medical examination. At this stage he applies for exemption from military service if he comes under one or more of the above categories.

One year later, when all the preliminaries are finished, the recruiting offices send for the conscripts (called *mozos*) of the draft (*quinta*), and they are then allotted to their regiments : infantry, cavalry, etc.

A certain number of men from each call-up are sent to do service in Spanish Morocco. These men are selected by a system of drawing lots.

Although the service is officially supposed to last two years, in fact, after eighteen months the men are sent home on indefinite leave and when the two years are up, they receive official confirmation that they have completed their military service. But up to the age of thirty-seven years they have to report once a year to the nearest military headquarters to have their army card stamped.

To enter the Navy a man has to sign on at the nearest naval headquarters when he becomes twenty, and his service will begin when he is twenty-one (that is, one year earlier than in the Army).

To enter the Air Force a man has to apply also before being called to the ranks (*llamado a filas*). To be selected he should be a photographer, a mechanic, an electrician ; in fact he should have a trade which is useful in the Air Force.

ARMY, NAVY, AIR FORCE	EJÉRCITO, MARINA, AVIACIÓN
Vocabulary	**Vocabulario**
THE ARMY	**EL EJÉRCITO**
The soldier	El soldado
The rank and file	La tropa
The regular	El voluntario
The conscript	El recluta
The infantry	La infantería
The artillery	La artillería
The engineers	Los ingenieros
The arms, weapons	Las armas, el armamento
The automatic rifle	El fusil-ametralladora
The bayonet	La bayoneta
The machine-gun	La ametralladora
The gun	El cañón
The (heavy) howitzer	El obús (pesado)
The grenade, shell	La granada
The ammunition	La munición
The flame-thrower	El lanzallamas
The mortar	El mortero
The rocket	El cohete
The atom bomb	La bomba atómica
The hydrogen bomb	La bomba de hidrógeno
The (armoured) tank	El tanque (blindado)
The camouflage	El camuflaje
The army of occupation	El ejército de ocupación
The town major	El comandante militar de la plaza
The parade, march past	El desfile
The barracks	El cuartel
The garrison	La guarnición
To salute	Saludar
The War Office	El Ministerio de la Guerra

Ranks :	Los grados :
The private	El soldado raso
The trooper	El soldado de caballería
The signaller	El soldado de transmisiones
The gunner	El artillero
The sapper	El zapador
The orderly	El asistente
The lance-corporal	El soldado de primera
The corporal	El cabo
The sergeant	El sargento
The company quartermaster-sergeant	El brigada
The second lieutenant	El alférez
The lieutenant	El teniente
The captain	El capitán
The major	El comandante
The lieutenant-colonel	El teniente coronel
The colonel	El coronel
The major-general	El general de brigada
The lieutenant-general	El general de división
The general	El teniente general
The field-marshal	El capitán general

THE NAVY   LA MARINA

The fleet	La armada, la flota
The man-of-war	El buque de guerra
The battleship	El acorazado
The cruiser	El crucero
The destroyer	El destructor
The motor torpedo-boat	La lancha torpedera
The submarine	El submarino
The mine-sweeper	El dragaminas
The gunboat	El cañonero
The torpedo	El torpedo
The depth charge	La carga de profundidad
The range	El alcance
The tonnage	El tonelaje

The convoy	El convoy
The sea-battle	La batalla naval
The port, harbour	El puerto
To sink	Hundir
To scuttle	Echar a pique
To rescue	Salvar
The Admiralty	El Ministerio de Marina

Ranks :	Los grados :
The ordinary seaman	El marinero
The able seaman	El marinero de primera
The stoker	El fogonero
The telegraphist	El telegrafista
The petty officer	El maestre
The chief petty officer	El contramaestre
The warrant officer	El condestable
The midshipman	El guardiamarina
The sub-lieutenant	El alférez de fragata
The lieutenant	El alférez de navío
The lieutenant-commander	El capitán de corbeta
The commander	El capitán de fragata
The captain	El capitán de navío
The commodore	El comodoro
The rear-admiral	El contraalmirante
The vice-admiral	El vicealmirante
The admiral	El almirante

THE AIR FORCE / LA AVIACIÓN

The airman	El aviador
The pilot	El piloto
The wireless operator	El radiotelegrafista
The crew	La tripulación
The fighter	El avión de caza
The bomber	El avión de bombardeo
The jet plane	El avión de propulsión a chorro
The helicopter	El autogiro
The glider	El planeador

The incendiary bomb	La bomba incendiaria
The reconnaissance flight	El vuelo de reconocimiento
The air-raid	La incursión aérea
The attack	El ataque
The A.R.P. Civil Defence	La defensa antiaérea
The ground personnel	El personal de tierra
The tarmac, landing strip	La pista de aterrizaje
The aerodrome	El aeródromo
The airfield	El campo de aviación
The balloon barrage	La barrera de globos
The squadron	La escuadrilla
To take off	Despegar
To land	Aterrizar, tomar tierra
To crash	Estrellarse
To shoot down a plane	Derribar un avión
To dive	Entrar en picado
Air Ministry	El Ministerio del Aire

Ranks :	Los grados :
The aircraftman	El soldado de aviación
The leading aircraftman	El soldado de aviación de primera
The corporal	El cabo
The sergeant	El sargento
The warrant officer	El brigada
The pilot officer	El alférez
The flying officer	El teniente
The flight-lieutenant	El capitán de escuadrilla
The squadron-leader	El comandante
The wing-commander	El teniente coronel
The group captain	El coronel, comandante de grupo
The air commodore	El general de brigada
The air vice-marshal	El general de división
The air-marshal	El teniente general
The air-chief-marshal	El capitán general

GENERAL VOCABULARY FOR LAND, SEA AND AIR FORCES

VOCABULARIO GENERAL PARA LOS EJÉRCITOS DE TIERRA, MAR Y AIRE

The war	La guerra
The battle	La batalla
The battle-field	El campo de batalla
The front	El frente
The rear, rear-guard	La retaguardia
The no-man's-land	La tierra de nadie
The victory	La victoria
The defeat	La derrota
The truce	La tregua
The armistice	El armisticio
The peace treaty	El tratado de paz
The prisoner of war	El prisionero de guerra
The hostage	El rehén
The camp	El campo
The casualties	Las bajas
To call up, mobilise	Movilizar
To demobilise	Licenciar
To serve	Servir, hacer el servicio
To fight	Combatir, pelear
To attack	Atacar
To defend	Defender
To shoot	Disparar
To invade	Invadir
To retreat	Retroceder, retirarse
To conquer	Conquistar

Phrases

Frases

Were you in the army?	¿ Perteneció usted al ejército ?
In which branch of the service were you?	¿ En qué cuerpo sirvió usted ?
I served with the engineers	Serví en ingenieros
I was a private in an armoured formation	Era soldado raso de una columna blindada
What is your miliary rank?	¿ Cuál es su grado militar ?

I am an officer	Soy oficial
How long were you in the army?	¿ Cuánto tiempo permaneció usted en el ejército ?
I joined up three years ago	Me alisté hace tres años
Were you called up?	¿ Le movilizaron ?
I volunteered	Fuí voluntario
We took the fortress by storm	Tomamos la fortaleza al asalto
They established a bridgehead	Establecieron una cabeza de puente
The enemy is in full retreat	El enemigo está en plena retirada
The army was defeated (annihilated)	El ejército fué derrotado (aniquilado)
Were you decorated in the war?	¿ Le han decorado durante la guerra ?
Were you wounded?	¿ Fué usted herido ?
Were you in a field-hospital?	¿ Estuvo usted en algún hospital de guerra ?
In which hospital were you?	¿ En qué hospital estuvo usted ?
He is disabled	Es mutilado
I am invalided out	Tengo permiso de convalecencia
I am going on leave	Me voy con permiso
He is demobilised	Le han licenciado
He is fit (unfit) for service	Es útil (inútil) para el servicio
How long did your training last?	¿ Cuánto tiempo duró su entrenamiento ?
Had you access to Headquarters?	¿ Tenía usted acceso al Cuartel General ?
I was a prisoner of war	Fuí prisionero de guerra
When were you taken prisoner?	¿ Cuándo le cogieron prisionero ?
I served in the navy	Serví en la marina
Were you a submarine captain?	¿ Fué usted capitán de submarino ?
Which was your naval base?	¿ Cuál era su base naval ?
I was a lieutenant on a cruiser	Fuí alférez de navío en un crucero

The ship was sunk, the crew was saved	El barco se hundió, la tripulación se salvó
How many men-of-war are lying in the harbour?	¿ Cuántos barcos de guerra hay en el puerto ?
The fleet has put out to sea	La flota se ha hecho a la mar
I am an airman	Soy aviador
Did you ever take part in an air-raid?	¿ Tomó usted parte en alguna incursión aérea ?
I belonged to the ground staff	Pertenecía al personal de tierra
I was a paratrooper	Fuí parachutista
He was sent out on patrol flights over the enemy country	Se le mandó a efectuar vuelos de patrulla sobre terreno enemigo
I made a few flights by night	Hice unos cuantos vuelos nocturnos
How long did you serve in the W.R.N.S.?	¿ Cuánto tiempo ha servido usted en el servicio auxiliar femenino de la marina ?
I joined the A.T.S. at the beginning of the war	Me alisté en el servicio auxiliar femenino del ejército al principio de la guerra
She is an officer in the W.A.A.F.	Ella es oficial del servicio auxiliar femenino de las fuerzas aéreas
My sister is a Red Cross nurse	Mi hermana es enfermera de la Cruz Roja

AN OUTLINE OF SPANISH GRAMMAR

As the title implies, this does not profess to be an exhaustive treatment of Spanish Grammar. Readers interested in the details and subtleties of grammar are recommended to refer to Mr. Scarlyn Wilson's book, " Teach Yourself Spanish ", where the grammar has been dealt with more thoroughly.

This outline, however, is detailed enough for the ordinary traveller who wishes to " get on " in Spain.

In an attempt to keep only essentials, some apparent inaccuracies may have crept in; we hope that the critical student will be indulgent. For instance, in saying that nouns ending in -*a* (except *el día, el mapa* and *el telegrama*) are feminine, we are not strictly accurate, but we feel that a list of unimportant exceptions would be out of place in a Phrase Book.

NOUNS

1. *Gender of Nouns :* As in French, nouns are either masculine or feminine. Nouns referring to males are obviously masculine, those referring to females are obviously feminine. The best way to learn the gender of a noun is to learn it with the article in the first place; e.g., *el lápiz* NOT *lápiz*. However, these elementary rules are useful to remember.

(1) Nouns ending in -*o* are masculine.

    e.g., *el libro, el río, el amigo*
    (Exceptions : *la mano, la radio*)

(2) Nouns ending in -*a* are feminine.

    e.g., *la ventana, la mesa*
    (Exceptions : *el día, el mapa, el telegrama*)

(3) Nouns ending in -*d*, -*ión*, and -*z*, are feminine.

    e.g., *la verdad, la nación, la vez*
    (Exceptions : *el avión, el lápiz*)

(4) Many other nouns ending in a consonant and referring to things are masculine.

    e.g., *el tenedor, el papel, el reloj*

2. *Plural of Nouns :* To form the plural, add -*s* if the word ends in vowel, and add -*es* if the word ends in a consonant.

    e.g., *amigos, ventanas, calles*
         naciones, verdades, ingleses

ARTICLES

1. *Definite Article*

    " The " = *el* before a masculine singular noun.

        e.g., *el libro*

" The " = *la* before a feminine singular noun.[1]
> e.g., *la mesa*

" The " = *los* before a masculine plural noun.
> e.g., *los libros, los papeles*

" The " = *las* before a feminine plural noun.
> e.g., *las mesas, las naciones*

De (= of) combines with *el* to form *del* (= of the).
> e.g., *el autor del libro*, the author of the book

A (= to, at) combines with *el* to form *al* (= to, or at, the).
> e.g., *vamos al río*, we go to the river
> *llegamos al cine*, we arrive at the cinema

2. *Indefinite Article*

" A " (or " an ") = *un* before a masculine singular noun.
> e.g., *un libro*

" A " (or " an ") = *una* before a feminine singular noun.
> e.g., *una niña*

After a negative verb this indefinite article often disappears.
> e.g., *no tengo libro*

3. *Partitive Article*

The Spanish equivalent of " Some " (or " any ") is not usually needed.
> e.g., *compro libros*, I buy some books
> *no tengo dinero*, I haven't any money

ADJECTIVES

As in French, adjectives agree in number and gender with the noun they qualify.

(a) If an adjective ends in *-o*, its feminine form will end in *-a*.
> e.g., *el libro rojo*, the red book
> *la casa roja*, the red house

The masculine plural form is *-os*, the feminine plural is *-as*.
> e.g., *los libros rojos*, the red books
> *las casas rojas*, the red houses

---

[1] If the first syllable of the feminine singular noun is a stressed *a* or *ha*, the article becomes *el*.
> e.g., *el agua*, water; *el hacha*, axe

(b) If an adjective ends in a consonant, its feminine form will be the same.

> e.g., *el libro difícil*, the difficult book
> *la lección difícil*, the difficult lesson

It will form its plural by adding *-es*.

> e.g., *los libros difíciles*, the difficult books
> *las lecciones difíciles*, the difficult lessons

N.B. Adjectives of nationality and those ending in *-an*, *-ón* and *-or* have a feminine form.

> e.g., *el libro inglés*, the English book
> *los libros ingleses*, the English books
> *la casa inglesa*, the English house
> *las casas inglesas*, the English houses
> *el hombre hablador*, the talkative man
> *la mujer habladora*, the talkative woman

Position of Adjectives

Most adjectives follow the noun, but there is no hard-and-fast rule. The adjectives *bueno*, *malo*, *uno*, *alguno*, *ninguno*, *primero*, *tercero* drop the final *o* when, as is usual, they precede the noun.

> e.g., *el buen libro*, the good book
> *el niño bueno*, the good child
> *el primer diente*, the first tooth
> *el capítulo primero*, the first chapter

The adjective *grande* drops *-de* before a singular noun whether masculine or feminine. The numeral *ciento* drops *-to* unless it is followed by another numeral.

> e.g., *una gran reina*, a great queen
> but
> *una casa grande*, a large house
> *cien personas*, one hundred people
> but
> *ciento cinco pesetas*, one hundred and five pesetas

Comparison of Adjectives

The comparative forms are formed by the insertion of *más* (more) and *menos* (less) before the adjective, (*que* is used for " than " if needed).

e.g., *Este libro es* $\begin{cases} \textit{más} \text{ (more) } \textit{importante que el de Luis} \\ \textit{menos} \text{ (less) } \textit{importante que el de Luis} \end{cases}$

Esta casa es $\begin{cases} \textit{más} \text{ (more) } \textit{antigua que las otras} \\ \textit{menos} \text{ (less) } \textit{antigua que las otras} \end{cases}$

There are four common irregular comparatives, viz. :

bueno, good ; *mejor*, better
malo, bad ; *peor*, worse
grande, big ; *mayor*, senior or older
pequeño, small ; *menor*, junior or younger

N.B. *más grande* = larger in size; *más pequeño* = smaller in size.

Equality is indicated by *tan . . . como*.

e.g., *Esta casa es* **tan** *antigua* **como** *la otra ;* This house is as old as the other.

Superlative of Adjectives

(*a*) The *relative superlative* is formed by inserting the corresponding definite article before the comparative form.

e.g., *Este libro es* **el más grande** *de mi biblioteca ;* This book is the biggest in my library.

Esta casa es **la más antigua** *de la ciudad ;* This house is the oldest in the town.

Juanito es **el menor** *de la familia ;* Johnny is the youngest member of the family.

But this is not possible if there is already one article and the adjective is placed before or just after the noun. In this case no article precedes the superlative form.

e.g., *El libro más interesante es la Biblia ;* The most interesting book is the Bible.

(*b*) The *absolute superlative* is formed by using *muy* (very) before the adjective; or by adding *-ísimo* (*-ísima*, etc.) to the adjective after removing the final vowel.

> e.g., *Es una traducción muy difícil.*
> *Es una traducción dificilísima.*
> It is a very difficult translation.

Possessive Adjectives

In Spanish, as in French, the possessive adjective agrees with the noun it qualifies.

	Singular.		Plural.	
my	*mi libro*	*mi casa*	*mis libros*	*mis casas*
thy	*tu libro*	*tu casa*	*tus libros*	*tus casas*
his her your [1]	*su libro*	*su casa*	*sus libros*	*sus casas*
our	*nuestro libro*	*nuestra casa*	*nuestros libros*	*nuestras casas*
your	*vuestro libro*	*vuestra casa*	*vuestros libros*	*vuestras casas*
their your	*su libro*	*su casa*	*sus libros*	*sus casas*

[1] See use of *usted*, p. 218.

Demonstrative Adjectives

The Spanish have three forms of demonstrative adjectives :

> (1) this, meaning this (here), *este*
> (2) that, meaning that (nearby), *ese*
> (3) that, meaning that (over there), *aquel*

	Singular.	
este libro	*esta casa*	this
ese libro	*esa casa*	this or that
aquel libro	*aquella casa*	that (over there)
	Plural.	
estos libros	*estas casas*	these
esos libros	*esas casas*	these or those
aquellos libros	*aquellas casas*	those (over there)

PRONOUNS

Demonstrative Pronouns

These are spelt like the demonstrative adjectives, but require an accent on the stressed syllables to distinguish them from the adjectives.

They mean " this one ", " that one ", " that one over there ".

> e.g., *Este libro es más agradable que* **ése** (that one)
>
> *Ese libro no es tan aburrido como* **aquél** (that one over there)

In addition there is a neuter form of demonstrative pronoun referring to ideas, statements which obviously have no gender (French *ceci, cela*).

> e.g., ¿ *Qué es esto ?* (¿ *eso ?, ¿ aquello ?*) ; What is this?
>
> *Eso es ;* That's right, that's it

Before a relative clause or *de* the demonstrative pronoun is usually replaced by *el, la, los* and *las.*

> e.g., *Esta casa y* **la** *de mi hermano son antiguas ;* This house and my brother's are old.
>
> *Aquel libro y* **los que** *tengo en casa son difíciles ;* That book and those I have at home are difficult.

The neuter form of this is *lo*, and so the English " what " (that which, etc.) is *lo que.*

> e.g., *No sabe* **lo que** *tengo ;* He does not know what I have.

Possessive Pronouns

These mean " mine ", " thine ", " ours ", " yours ", " theirs ", etc.

	Singular.		Plural.	
	Masculine.	*Feminine.*	*Masculine.*	*Feminine.*
mine	*el mío*	*la mía*	*los míos*	*las mías*
thine	*el tuyo*	*la tuya*	*los tuyos*	*las tuyas*
his hers yours }	*el suyo*	*la suya*	*los suyos*	*las suyas*
ours	*el nuestro*	*la nuestra*	*los nuestros*	*las nuestras*
yours	*el vuestro*	*la vuestra*	*los vuestros*	*las vuestras*
theirs, masc. theirs, fem. yours, plural }	*el suyo*	*la suya*	*los suyos*	*as suyas*

> e.g., *Este libro no es tan interesante como* **el mío** *;* This book is not so interesting as *mine.*
>
> *Nuestra casa y* **la suya** *son antiguas ;* Our house and *his* are old.

N.B. (1) The article can be omitted when the pronoun is a predicate object of the verb *ser* (to be).

e.g., *Esta casa es mía ;* This house is mine.

(2) *El suyo, la suya,* etc., has six possible meanings (his, hers, yours (sing.), theirs (masc.), theirs (fem.), yours (plural)), and often requires the substitution of *de él* (his), *de ella* (hers), *de usted* (yours sing.), *de ellos* (theirs masc.), *de ellas* (theirs fem.), *de ustedes* (yours plural), to avoid ambiguity.

e.g., *Esta casa es la de ella, no la de él;* This house is hers, not his.

Personal Pronouns

Subject.	Object.	Indirect Object.	Direct–Indirect Reflexive Object.	Disjunctive Separated.
1	2	3	4	5
yo	me	me	me	mí
tú	te	te	te	ti
él	lo	le	se	él
ella	la	la or le	se	ella
usted	lo or la	le or la	se	usted
nosotros	nos	nos	nos	nosotros
vosotros	os	os	os	vosotros
ellos	los	les	se	ellos
ellas	las	las or les	se	ellas
ustedes	los or las	les or las	se	ustedes

(a) *Use of Usted.* *Usted,* written sometimes *Vd.,* *Ud.* or *V.,* comes from the old Spanish *vuestra merced,* meaning " your honour ", and hence is treated as a third person pronoun with its plural *ustedes.* It is the normal form of address, except to close friends and relations, when *tú* and *vosotros* are used. A common greeting is :

¿ Cómo está usted ? (Literally, How is your honour ?) How are you ?

(b) *Use of Subject Pronouns* (Column 1). As in Spanish the ending of the verb indicates the subject, e.g., *hablo = I speak,* the subject pronouns are used only for emphasis. *Usted* and

ustedes, however, are often inserted to avoid ambiguity with the other third person pronouns, as well as to show respect and politeness to the person addressed.

> e.g., *¿ Cómo está usted ?*   How are you ?
>
> *¿ Adónde van ustedes ?*   Where are you going ?

(c) *The Position and Order of the Object Pronouns* (Columns 2, 3, 4). Normally the object pronouns precede the verb. When two pronouns of Columns 2, 3 and 4 are governed by the same verb the pronoun from Column 2 comes last.

> e.g., *(Él)* **me lo** *lee ;*   He reads it to me.
>
> *(Él) no* **nos los** *ha leído ;*   He has not read them to us.

But when the verb is (1) an infinitive, (2) a gerund, or (3) a positive command, the pronouns are joined to the end of the verb.

> e.g., *Antes de leer***lo** *;*   Before reading it.
>
> *Leyéndo***lo** *;*   While reading it.
>
> *Léa***lo** *usted ;*   Read it.

Of course, *No* **lo** *lea ;*   Don't read it (a negative command).

(d) *Substitution of* se *for* le, la, les *or* las.   *Le, la, les* or *las* become *se* when followed immediately by *lo, los, la, las* of Column 2. The pronouns in Column 5 are then sometimes needed to indicate which pronoun has been substituted.

> e.g., *Se lo leo* can have six meanings :
>
> *Se lo leo a él ;*   I read it to him.
>
> *Se lo leo a ella ;*   I read it to her.
>
> *Se lo leo a usted ;*   I read it to you (sing.).
>
> *Se lo leo a ellos ;*   I read it to them (masc.).
>
> *Se lo leo a ellas ;*   I read it to them (fem.).
>
> *Se lo leo a ustedes ;*   I read it to you (plural).

Similarly,

> *Quiero dárselo a él ;*   I want to give it to him.
>
> *Quiero dárselo a usted,* etc.;   I want to give it to you, etc.

and,

> *Léaselo a él ;* Read it to him.
> *Léaselo a ellas ;* Read it to them, (fem.)

(e) *Other uses of* se. *Se* is also used.

(1) As an ordinary reflexive pronoun—

> e.g., *Ellos se lavan ;* They wash themselves.
> *Él se levanta ;* He gets up.

(2) To avoid the passive voice—

> e.g., *Se venden libros ;* Books are sold.

(3) To form a kind of impersonal verb—

> e.g., *Se dice que . . . ;* It is said that .
> *Se me dice que . . .;* I am told that . . . (literally, it is said to me . . .)

(f) *Use of Pronouns in Column 5.* These are separated from the verb and are most frequently found after prepositions usually for the sake of emphasis or, as mentioned in (d) above, to avoid ambiguity.

> e.g., *A mí, me lo ha leído ;* He has read it *to me.*
> *A usted, le gusta leer ;* *You* like reading.
> *Se lo leo a ella, no a usted ;* I'm reading it *to her,* not to you.
> *Han salido sin ella ;* They have gone out without *her.*

N.B. *Conmigo* = with me; *contigo* = with you; *consigo* = with himself, herself, oneself.

> e.g., *Vendrán conmigo ;* They will come with me.

Relative Pronouns (Who, Which, etc.)

		Persons.		Things.
Subject	que	(who)	que	(which)
Object	que	(whom)	que	(which)
Whose	cuyo	(-a, -os, -as)	cuyo	(-a, -os, -as)
Prepositional	de	} quien(-es)	de	} que (which)
Simple prepositions	a con, etc.	(whom)	a con, etc.	

e.g., *El libro que compro*, the book which I buy

El hombre que canta, the man who is singing

El libro de que hablamos, the book we are talking about

El hombre de quien hablo, the man I am talking about

Los soldados con quienes viajé, the soldiers with whom I travelled

(1) *Use of* el cual, la cual, los cuales, las cuales. These are normally used instead of *que* (which) when it is governed by *por*, *sin* or a preposition of more than one syllable.

e.g., *La casa hacia la cual nos dirigimos*, the house we are making for (literally, the house towards which we are directing ourselves)

These are also used, instead of *que* or *quien(-es)*, to avoid ambiguity.

e.g., *La hermana de mi amigo* $\begin{Bmatrix} \text{que} \\ \text{la cual} \end{Bmatrix}$ *es tan feliz*

(2) *Use of* cuyo, cuya, cuyos, cuyas = *whose*. *Cuyo* is really an adjective, and agrees in number and gender with the noun which follows.

e.g., *El hombre **cuya casa** he comprado*, the man whose house I have bought

N.B. Cuyo is rarely found as an interrogative adjective. *De quién* takes its place.

e.g., *¿ De quién es el libro ?* Whose book is it ?

(3) *Lo que* (what) is a relative.

e.g., *No sé lo que ha hecho ;* I don't know what he has done.

Lo que más me gusta es la cocina española ; What I prefer is Spanish cooking.

Lo que (or *lo cual*) is also used to translate *which* when it refers to a previous idea or statement.

e.g., *Mi amigo no habla mucho*, **lo que** *me agrada ;* My friend does not speak much, which pleases me.

Interrogative Pronouns (*Who ? Whom ? What ? Which one ?*)

Who ? *¿ Quién ?*
What ? *¿ Qué ?*
Whom ? *¿ A quién ?*
Which one ? *¿ Cuál(-es) ?*

Notice the accent which is used to signify the interrogative form.

e.g., *¿ A quién habla usted ?* To whom are you speaking ?

¿ Con quiénes visitaron el museo ? With whom did they visit the museum ?

¿ Qué come usted ? What do you eat ?

¿ Qué hizo su hermano ? What did your brother do ?

¿ De qué está hablando ? What is he talking about ?

¿ Cuál es su libro ? Which is his book ?

¿ Cuáles de los libros prefiere usted ? Which of the books do you prefer ?

Interrogative Adjectives (*What ? Which ?* = *¿* Qué ?)

e.g., *¿ Qué hora es ?* What's the time.

¿ Qué libros leyó usted ? What (which) books did you read ?

¿ De qué ciudad es usted ? Which town do you come from ?

How much ? = *¿ cuánto(-a) ?* How many ? = *¿ cuántos(-as) ?*

e.g., *¿ Cuánto es ?* How much is it ?

¿ Cuántas hermanas tiene usted ? How many sisters have you ?

Indefinite Adjectives and Pronouns

Positive.	Negative.
alguien, somebody	*nadie*, nobody
algo, something	*nada*, nothing
alguno(-a, -os, -as), some, a few	*ninguno(-a, -os, -as)*, none
mucho(-a, -os, -as), much, many	*poco(-a, -os, -as)*, little, few

When the negatives are placed after the verb, *no* must be inserted in its normal position.

e.g., *No como nada ;* I don't eat anything.

No viene nadie ; Nobody is coming.

When the negatives precede the verb, *no* is omitted.

e.g., *Yo nada leo ;* I read nothing.

Nadie viene ; Nobody comes.

Other useful indefinites are :

una cosa, a thing	*todo*, everything
otra cosa, something else	*todos*, everybody
ambos(-as), both	*todo el mundo*, everybody
los(-as) dos, both	*tal*, such
cada, each	*un tal*, a certain
cada uno(-a), each one	*cierto*, certain
cada cual, each one	*mismo*, same, self
otro, another	

SOME COMMON PREPOSITIONS

A means " to ", " at " and, sometimes, " from ".

(*a*) It is used after verbs of motion to mean " to ".

e.g., *Vamos a Madrid ;* We are going to Madrid.

La gente corre a ver el accidente ; The people are running to see the accident.

(*b*) It is used after verbs of beginning, preparing and teaching, to introduce the infinitive which follows.

e.g., *Empezamos a bailar ;* We began to dance.

Aprendo a hablar español ; I am learning to speak Spanish.

(*c*) It is used after verbs indicating separation and often means " from " in this position.

e.g., *Compré este libro a un amigo ;* I bought this book from a friend.

Robó el dinero a su tío ; He stole the money from his uncle.

And, of course,

Entregaron la carta al profesor ; They handed the letter to the teacher.

(*d*) It is inserted before expressions of distance.

> e.g., *La casa está* **a** *cinco kilómetros de la ciudad ;* The house is five kilometres from the town.

(*e*) *Personal A* is used to introduce a personal object, direct or indirect.

> e.g., *Jorge va a visitar* **a** *su tía ;* George is going to visit his aunt.
>
> *Hoy hemos visto* **a** *la Reina ;* We saw the Queen to-day.
>
> *El profesor enseña el español a su clase ;* The teacher teaches Spanish to his class (*or* his class Spanish).
>
> *Regalaré un libro a mi hermano ;* I shall give my brother a book.

Con means " with ".

> e.g., *Vive con nosotros ;* He is living with us.

Here are a few idiomatic uses:
soñar con = to dream of

> e.g., *Sueño con mis vacaciones ;* I dream of my holiday.

casarse con alguien = to marry someone

> *Ella va a casarse con el hijo de mi amigo ;* She is going to marry my friend's son.

contar con = to rely on

> *El padre cuenta con el dinero de su mujer ;* The father relies on his wife's money.

N.B. See page 220 for use of *conmigo, contigo,* etc., and page 227 for use of *con* with nouns to form adverbs.

De means " of ", " from ", and indicates possession.

> e.g., *Estoy comprando una libra de manteca ;* I am buying a pound of butter.
>
> *El tren llega de Madrid a las diez ;* The train arrives from Madrid at ten o'clock.
>
> *La casa de mi abuelo ;* My grandfather's house.

It is also used after verbs of ending and other verbs, to introduce the infinitive which follows.

> e.g., *Cesaron de trabajar ;* They stopped working.
>
> *Acaba de llegar ;* He has just arrived.
>
> *Trataré de levantarme temprano ;* I'll try to get up early.

En means " in ", " on ", " at ", and indicates " place where ".

> e.g., *Estamos en Londres, en Inglaterra ;* We are in London, in England.
>
> *No ponga usted el mantel en la mesa ;* Do not put the tablecloth on the table.
>
> *Nos veremos en el parque ;* We shall meet in the park.

It also has the following idiomatic uses :

Pensar en algo (alguien), to think of something (someone)

> e.g., *Piensan en su dinero ;* They are thinking of their money.
>
> *Estaba pensando en usted ahora mismo ;* I was just thinking of you.

Tardar en hacer algo, to be slow in doing something.

> e.g., *El médico no tardó en venir a verle ;* The doctor was not slow in coming to see him (or soon came to see him).

Ocuparse en (hacer) algo, to be busy in doing something.

> e.g., *Ella se ocupaba en cocinar ;* She was busy cooking.

Para means " in order to ", " to ", " for " (see below).

> e.g., *Come para vivir ;* He eats (in order) to live.
>
> *Habla para sí ;* He is talking to himself.

Por means " by ", " through ", " for " (see below).

> e.g., *Pasaron por la calle principal ;* They went through the main street.
>
> *Fué atropellado por un automóvil ;* He was run over by a car.
>
> *Por avión,* by air

H

Both these prepositions mean "for", and the following columns should help to indicate the common uses of *para* and *por*.

Para.

(1) Destination.

e.g., *El tren sale para Madrid ;* The train is leaving for Madrid.

(2) Suitability for.

e.g., *Es alto para su edad ;* He is tall for his age.

(3) Purpose.

e.g., *Compro el libro para mi madre ;* I buy the book for my mother.

(4) Limit of future time.

e.g., *Estarán preparados para el domingo ;* They will be ready for Sunday.

Por.

(1) Exchange.

e.g., *Di dos pesetas por el libro ;* I gave two pesetas for the book.

(2) Reason for, because of, through.

e.g., *Por eso no voy ;* That is why I am not going.

Por miedo, for fear

(3) In favour of, on behalf of.

e.g., *Murió por su patria ;* He died for his country.

Habló por sus colegas de trabajo ; He spoke for his colleagues.

But other phrases which cannot be classified easily are best learnt as they occur.

e.g., *Preguntó por Carlos ;* He asked (to see) for Carlos.

Mañana por la mañana, por la tarde, etc.; To-morrow morning, afternoon, etc.

Estamos para salir ; We are about to leave.

ADVERBS

Position. The usual practice is to place adverbs immediately after the verb; although short adverbs of time, like *hoy, ayer, ya*, etc., frequently stand first in the sentence.

> e.g., *Hablaba despacio ;* He was speaking slowly.
> *Ayer me tropecé con él ;* I met him yesterday.

Formation : (*a*) Add *-mente* to the feminine form of the adjective to form some adverbs of manner.

> e.g., *Intenso, -a, intensamente*
> *loco, -a, locamente*
> *considerable, considerablemente*

(*b*) Sometimes *con* plus a noun is used to form an adverb.

> e.g., *silenciosamente* or *con silencio*
> *cuidadosamente* or *con cuidado*

N.B. The *-mente* ending is removed from the first adverb if two or more adverbs ending in *-mente* are used close to each other.

> e.g., *Escribe correcta y elegantemente ;* He writes correctly and elegantly.

Comparison of adverbs. This is achieved by using *más*, and *lo más* for the superlative.

> e.g., *Camina más despacio ;* Walk more slowly.

Note these irregular comparisons :

well, *bien ;*	better, *mejor ;*	best, *lo mejor*
badly, *mal ;*	worse, *peor;*	worst, *lo peor*
much, *mucho ;*	more, *más ;*	most, *lo más*
little, *poco ;*	less, *menos ;*	least, *lo menos*

Some *common adverbs* are :

siempre, always	*desde luego*, of course
acaso, perhaps	*despacio*, slowly
en seguida, immediately	*de prisa*, fast
de nuevo, again	*tampoco*, neither
bastante, enough	*claro*, evidently

demasiado, too (much)   *todavía*, still
a menudo, often   *pronto*, soon
a veces, sometimes

These should be learnt off by heart, and the list extended regularly.

VERBS

Infinitive

The Infinitive (e.g., to do, to sing, etc.) ends in

-ar, e.g., *cantar*, to sing
-er, e.g., *comer*, to eat, or
-ir, e.g., *vivir*, to live

But outside the first and second person plural of the Present Tense and the Familiar Plural Imperative, the verbs ending in *-er* and *-ir* are conjugated similarly.

Like a noun, the Infinitive can be used as a subject of a verb. It is always masculine, and sometimes has the article *el* in front.

e.g., *Me gusta (el) viajar* ; I like travelling (to travel) (Literally : (To) travel gives me pleasure).
Hablar idiomas es útil ; It is useful to speak languages.

When a Spanish verb is governed by a preposition it is almost always in the infinitive mood.

e.g., *Después de hablar*, after talking
Llegó sin ver a nadie ; He arrived without seeing anyone.

Participles

The Present Participle (or Gerund) of *-ar* verbs ends in *-ando*, and that of the *-er* and *-ir* verbs in *-iendo*.

The Past Participles end in *-ado* and *-ido*, respectively.

e.g., *hablar*, to speak; *hablando*, speaking; *hablado*, spoken
comer, to eat; *comiendo*, eating; *comido*, eaten
vivir, to live; *viviendo*, living; *vivido*, lived

(a) The *Present Participle* is used :

(1) With the verb *estar* (and sometimes *ir*, to go, and *seguir*, to follow) to form continuous tenses.

> e.g., *estoy escribiendo*, I am writing
> *están comiendo*, they are eating
> *siguen jugando*, they go on playing

(2) To translate the English " by ", " while ", " through " with the Present Participle form.

> e.g., *Trabajando mucho, ganará mucho dinero ;* By working hard, you will earn a lot of money.

Some common irregular Present Participles to be learnt are :

> *decir, diciendo*, saying   *oír, oyendo*, saying
> *ir, yendo*, going   *poder, pudiendo*, being able
> *venir, viniendo*, coming

(b) The *Past Participle* is used :

(1) With the verb *haber* to form compound tenses.

> e.g., *he hablado*, I have spoken
> *habían comido*, they had eaten

(2) With the verb *ser* to form the passive voice, in which case the Past Participle agrees with the subject.

> e.g., *fueron asesinados ;* they were assassinated
> *ha sido aplaudida ;* she has been applauded

(3) With the verb *estar* to express a state or condition resulting from previous action. Here, too, the Past Participle agrees with the subject.

> e.g., *estamos sentados ;* we are seated (sitting down)
> *estaba cansada ;* she was tired

Some common irregular Past Participles which should be learnt with their compounds are :

> *abrir, abierto*, opened   *morir, muerto*, dead
> *cubrir, cubierto*, covered   *poner, puesto*, placed, put
> *decir, dicho*, said, told   *romper, roto*, broken, torn

escribir, escrito, written	*ver, visto,* seen
hacer, hecho, made, done	*volver, vuelto,* returned
imprimir, impreso, printed	

Tenses

Present of Regular Verbs

Formation. Remove the ending *-ar, -er, -ir* and add to the stem of :

-ar verbs, *-o, -as, -a, -amos, -áis, -an.*

> e.g., *hablo,* I speak
> *hablas,* thou speakest
> *habla,* he speaks
> *hablamos,* we speak
> *habláis,* you speak
> *hablan,* they speak

-er verbs, *-o, -es, -e, -emos, -éis, -en.*

> e.g., *como,* I eat
> *comes,* thou eatest
> *come,* he eats
> *comemos,* we eat
> *coméis,* you eat
> *comen,* they eat

-ir verbs, *-o, -es, -e, -imos, -ís, -en.*

> e.g., *vivo,* I live
> *vives,* thou livest
> *vive,* he lives
> *vivimos,* we live
> *vivís,* you live
> *viven,* they live

Present Continuous

This is formed with *estar* and the Present Participle (see page 229).

Use. It is used to describe an action going on at the present time.

Imperative (Familiar, i.e., not with usted)

This is as follows :

Habla (tú)	*hablad (vosotros)*
Come (tú)	*comed (vosotros)*
Vive (tú)	*vivid (vosotros)*

Imperfect Tense

Formation. Remove the ending of the infinitive and add to the stem of :

    -ar verbs, *-aba, -abas, -aba, -ábamos, -abais, -aban.*

      e.g., *hablaba,* I was speaking
            hablabas, thou wast speaking
            hablaba, he was speaking
            hablábamos, we were speaking
            hablabais, you were speaking
            hablaban, they were speaking

   -er and *-ir* verbs, *-ía, -ías, -ía, -íamos, -íais, -ían.*

      e.g., *comía,* I was eating
             comías, thou wast eating
             comía, he was eating
             comíamos, we were eating
             comíais, you were eating
             comían, they were eating

             vivía, I was living
             vivías, thou wast living
             vivía, he was living
             vivíamos, we were living
             viviais, you were living
             vivían, they were living

Past Continuous

This is formed with Imperfect of *estar* and the Present Participle.

Use. It is used in writing and in conversation to express :

    (a) habitual actions (what used to happen) ;

(b) interrupted action (what was going on when something else happened);

(c) past description (e.g., the sky was blue, etc.).

*Past Historic (or Preterite or Past Definite, etc.) of Regular
Verbs*

Formation.   Remove the ending of the infinitive and add to
the stem of:

-*ar* verbs, -*é*, -*aste*, -*ó*, -*amos*, -*asteis*, -*aron*.

 e.g., *hablé*, I spoke
   hablaste, thou spokest
   habló, he spoke
   hablamos, we spoke
   hablasteis, you spoke
   hablaron, they spoke

-*er* and -*ir* verbs, -*í*, -*iste*, -*ió*, -*imos*, -*isteis*, -*ieron*.

 e.g., *comí*, I ate
   comiste, thou atest
   comió, he ate
   comimos, we ate
   comisteis, you ate
   comieron, they ate

   viví, I lived
   viviste, thou livest
   vivió, he lived
   vivimos, we lived
   vivisteis, you lived
   vivieron, they lived

N.B.   There is a group of verbs which have what are called
pretéritos graves.   They add -*e*, -*iste*, -*o*, -*imos*, -*isteis*, -*ieron* to
their irregular stem.   They are common verbs and should be
learnt.

  e.g., andar : anduve, anduviste, anduvo, anduvimos,
    anduvisteis, anduvieron, (*I walked, etc.*)
   caber : cupe, cupiste, cupo, cupimos, cupisteis,
    cupieron, (*I could be contained in, etc.*)

decir : dije, dijiste, dijo, dijimos, dijisteis, **dijeron,** (*I said, etc.*)

haber : hube, hubiste, hubo, hubimos, hubisteis, hubieron, (*I had, etc.*)

hacer : hice, hiciste, **hizo,** hicimos, hicisteis, hicieron, (*I made, etc.*)

estar : estuve, estuviste, estuvo, estuvimos, estuvisteis, estuvieron, (*I was, etc.*)

poder : pude, pudiste, pudo, pudimos, pudisteis, pudieron, (*I could, etc.*)

poner : puse, pusiste, puso, pusimos, pusisteis, pusieron, (*I put, etc.*)

querer : quise, quisiste, quiso, quisimos, quisisteis, quisieron, (*I wished, etc.*)

saber : supe, supiste, supo, supimos, supisteis, supieron, (*I knew, etc.*)

tener : tuve, tuviste, tuvo, tuvimos, tuvisteis, tuvieron, (*I had, etc.*)

traer : traje, trajiste, trajo, trajimos, trajisteis, **trajeron,** (*I brought, etc.*)

venir : vine, viniste, vino, vinimos, vinisteis, vinieron, (*I came, etc.*)

Use. The Past Historic is used in writing and in conversation to express :

(*a*) an action or an event, normally of definite duration, which took place in the past;

(*b*) an interrupting action;

(*c*) the events in a story.

The following sentences should help to distinguish some of the differences between the Imperfect and the Past Historic :

e.g., *Un poeta* **envió** *a un editor un poema titulado X ;* A poet sent (once) to a publisher a poem entitled X.

Poco después se lo **devolvieron** *con una nota que* **decía** . . .; Soon afterwards they sent it back to him with a note which said . . . (description of note).

Entré *en la sala de espera.* **Había** *una mesa, un banco y una silla ;* I entered (event) the waiting-room. There were (description) a table, a bench and a chair.

Durante un momento se **quedó** *pensativo ;* He remained pensive for a moment (definite duration).

Yo **vivía** *en París.* **Tenía** *un piso que* **daba** *al cementerio ;* I was living in Paris. I had a flat which looked on to the cemetery.

Los aldeanos que **regresaban** *a sus casas* **vieron** *una bola de fuego que* **caía** *de las nubes ;* The villagers were returning home when they saw (event) a ball of flame which was falling from the clouds.

Future Tense

Formation. Add to the infinitive the following endings *-é, -ás, -á, -emos, -éis, -án.*

e.g., *hablaré,* I shall speak
hablarás, thou wilt speak
hablará, he will speak
hablaremos, we shall speak
hablaréis, you will speak
hablarán, they will speak

comeré, I shall eat
comerás, thou wilt eat
comerá, he will eat
comeremos, we shall eat
comeréis, you will eat
comerán, they will eat

viviré, I shall live
vivirás, thou wilt live
vivirá, he will live
viviremos, we shall live
viviréis, you will live
vivirán, they will live

The following have an *irregular future stem* (the endings of the future are the same) :

decir : diré, dirás, dirá, diremos, diréis, dirán, (*I shall say, etc.*)

haber : habré, habrás, habrá, habremos, habréis, habrán, (*I shall have, etc.*)

hacer : haré, harás, hará, haremos, haréis, harán, (*I shall do, etc.*)

poder : podré, podrás, podrá, podremos, podréis, podrán, (*I shall be able, etc.*)

poner : pondré, pondrás, pondrá, pondremos, pondréis, pondrán, (*I shall put, etc.*)

querer : querré, querrás, querrá, querremos, querréis, querrán, (*I shall want, etc.*)

saber : sabré, sabrás, sabrá, sabremos, sabréis, sabrán, (*I shall know, etc.*)

salir : saldré, saldrás, saldrá, saldremos, saldréis, saldrán, (*I shall go out, etc.*)

tener : tendré, tendrás, tendrá, tendremos, tendréis, tendrán, (*I shall have, etc.*)

valer : valdré, valdrás, valdrá, valdremos, valdréis, valdrán, (*I shall be worth, etc.*)

venir : vendré, vendrás, vendrá, vendremos, vendréis, vendrán, (*I shall come, etc.*)

Use. As in English.

Conditional Tense

Formation. Add to the future stem of all verbs the following endings (which are, incidentally, the same endings as those used in the Imperfect Tense of *-er* and *-ir* verbs) : *-ía, -ías, -ía, -íamos, -íais, -ían.*

> e.g., *hablaría*, I should speak
> *hablarías*, thou wouldst speak
> *hablaría*, he would speak
> *hablaríamos*, we should speak
> *hablaríais*, you would speak
> *hablarían*, they would speak

comería, I should eat
comerías, thou wouldst eat
comería, he would eat
comeríamos, we should eat
comeríais, you would eat
comerían, they would eat

viviría, I should live
vivirías, thou wouldst live
viviría, he would live
viviríamos, we should live
viviríais, you should live
vivirían, they would live

And, of course, the irregular future stem will give :

decir : diría, dirías, diría, diríamos, diríais, dirían, (*I should say, etc.*)

haber : habría, habrías, habría, habríamos, habríais, habrían, (*I should have, etc.*)

hacer : haría, harías, haría, haríamos, haríais, harían, (*I should do, etc.*)

poder : podría, podrías, podría, podríamos, podríais, podrían, (*I should be able, etc.*)

poner : pondría, pondrías, pondría, pondríamos, pondríais, pondrían, (*I should put, etc.*)

querer : querría, querrías, querría, querríamos, querríais, querrían, (*I should want, etc.*)

saber : sabría, sabrías, sabría, sabríamos, sabríais, sabrían, (*I should know, etc.*)

salir : saldría, saldrías, saldría, saldríamos, saldríais, saldrían, (*I should go out, etc.*)

tener : tendría, tendrías, tendría, tendríamos, tendríais, tendrían, (*I should have, etc.*)

valer : valdría, valdrías, valdría, valdríamos, valdríais, valdrían, (*I should be worth, etc.*)

venir : vendría, vendrías, vendría, vendríamos, vendríais, vendrían, (*I should come, etc.*)

Use. As in English.

Perfect Tense

Formation. The Present Tense of *haber* used with the Past Participle (see page 229).

> e.g., **he** *hablado,* I have spoken
> **has** *hablado,* thou hast spoken
> **ha** *hablado,* he has spoken
> **hemos** *hablado,* we have spoken
> **habéis** *hablado,* you have spoken
> **han** *hablado,* they have spoken
>
> *he comido,* I have eaten
> *has comido,* thou hast eaten
> *ha comido,* he has eaten
> *hemos comido,* we have eaten
> *habéis comido,* you have eaten
> *han comido,* they have eaten
>
> *he vivido,* I have lived
> *has vivido,* thou hast lived
> *ha vivido,* he has lived
> *hemos vivido,* we have lived
> *habéis vivido,* you have lived
> *han vivido,* they have lived

Use. It is often used to express a finished event in a period of time still unfinished.

> e.g., *Hoy he visto a mis amigos ;* I have seen (saw) my friends to-day.
> *He ganado poco dinero este año ;* I have not earned much money this year.

The Pluperfect Tense

Formation. The Imperfect Tense of *haber* used with the Past Participle.

> e.g., **había** *hablado,* I had spoken
> **habías** *hablado,* thou hadst spoken
> **había** *hablado,* he had spoken
> **habíamos** *hablado,* we had spoken
> **habíais** *hablado,* you had spoken
> **habían** *hablado,* they had spoken

        había comido, I had eaten
        habías comido, thou hadst eaten
        había comido, he had eaten
        habíamos comido, we had eaten
        habíais comido, you had eaten
        habían comido, they had eaten

        había vivido, I had lived
        habías vivido, thou hadst lived
        había vivido, he had lived
        habíamos vivido, we had lived
        habíais vivido, you had lived
        habían vivido, they had lived

Use.   As in English.

The Past Anterior Tense
   Formation.   The Past Historic Tense of *haber* used with the Past Participle.

      e.g., **hube** *hablado*, I had spoken
           hubiste *hablado*, thou hadst spoken
           hubo *hablado*, he had spoken
           hubimos *hablado*, we had spoken
           hubisteis *hablado*, you had spoken
           hubieron *hablado*, they had spoken

           hube comido, I had eaten
           hubiste comido, thou hadst eaten
           hubo comido, he had eaten
           hubimos comido, we had eaten
           hubisteis comido, you had eaten
           hubieron comido, they had eaten

           hube vivido, I had lived
           hubiste vivido, thou hadst lived
           hubo vivido, he had lived
           hubimos vivido, we had lived
           hubisteis vivido, you had lived
           hubieron vivido, they had lived

Use. In temporal clauses (i.e., those introduced by the conjunctions *cuando, en cuanto, después que,* etc.) when the main verb is in the Past Historic.

> e.g., *Cuando hubieron llegado, nos fuimos a comer ;*
> When they had arrived we went to eat.

Subjunctive Mood

Present of Regular Verbs

Formation. -*ar* verbs : remove the -*o* of the first person singular of the Present Tense, and add : -*e, -es, -e, -emos, -éis, -en.*

> e.g., *hable,* I may speak (approx. meaning)
> *hables,* thou mayest speak
> *hable,* he may speak
> *hablemos,* we may speak
> *habléis,* you may speak
> *hablen,* they may speak

-*er* and -*ir* verbs : remove the -*o* of the first person singular of the Present Tense and add : -*a, -as, -a, -amos, -áis, -an.*

> e.g., *coma,* I may eat
> *comas,* thou mayest eat
> *coma,* he may eat
> *comamos,* we may eat
> *comáis,* you may eat
> *coman,* they may eat
>
> *viva,* I may live
> *vivas,* thou mayest live
> *viva,* he may live
> *vivamos,* we may live
> *viváis,* you may live
> *vivan,* they may live

Imperfect Subjunctive of all Verbs

This tense has two forms, but there is no difference either in meaning or use.

Formation. Remove the *-ron* of the third person plural of the Past Historic Tense and add : (a) *-ra, -ras, -ra, -ramos, -rais, -ran ;* or (b) *-se, -ses, -se, -semos, -seis, -sen.*

		Approx. meaning.
e.g., *hablara,*	*hablase*	I might speak
hablaras,	*hablases*	thou mightest speak
hablara,	*hablase*	he might speak
habláramos,	*hablásemos*	we might speak
hablarais,	*hablaseis*	you might speak
hablaran,	*hablasen*	they might speak
comiera,	*comiese*	I might eat
comieras,	*comieses*	thou mightest eat
comiera,	*comiese*	he might eat
comiéramos,	*comiésemos*	we might eat
comierais,	*comieseis*	you might eat
comieran,	*comiesen*	they might eat
viviera,	*viviese*	I might live
vivieras,	*vivieses*	thou mightest live
viviera,	*viviese*	he might live
viviéramos,	*viviésemos*	we might live
vivierais,	*vivieseis*	you might live
vivieran,	*viviesen*	they might live

Uses of the Subjunctive Tenses

Those readers who have never studied the Subjunctive Mood should consider the following points or general principles about its use. Those who have studied advanced French will notice some differences.

(1) It is used to express commands and requests. (Hence polite commands are always in the subjunctive mood.)

(2) It is used in clauses depending on verbs which express a conception of the mind. (Hence after verbs of emotion and supposition.)

(3) It is used in clauses which express what may happen at some future time—it is hardly ever used to state a definite fact.

(a) *In Main Clauses* the Subjunctive is used for all impera-
tives, except Positive Familiar Commands, and to express
wishes and prayers.

> e.g., *¡ Oiga Vd !* Listen ! I say !
> *¡ Viva la Reina !* Long live the Queen
> *¡ Vayan ustedes con Dios !* Good-bye, Farewell!
> *Siga leyendo ;* Go on reading.
> *¡ No lloréis !* Don't cry ! ⎫ (*Familiar negative*
> *¡ No lo bebas !* Don't drink it ! ⎭ *commands*)

(b) *In Dependent Clauses*, the Subjunctive is used as follows :

(1) Just as direct commands, wishes, requests require the
Subjunctive, so do indirect commands, etc. In other words, it
is used in clauses depending on verbs of ordering, requesting,
wishing and, of course, forbidding when the subject is different
from that of the main verb.

> e.g., *Dígale que se calle ;* Tell him to stop talking.
> *¿ Qué quiere usted que yo haga ?* What do you
> want me to do ?
> *Les rogaré que me ayuden ;* I'll ask them to help
> me.

(2) It is used in clauses depending on verbs of emotion (e.g.,
fear, joy, sorrow, surprise, hope, etc.).

> e.g., *Temo que no vengan ;* I'm afraid they are not
> coming.
> *Estamos contentos de que trabajen bien ;* We are
> glad they are working well.
> *Sienten que él se haya marchado ;* They are sorry
> he has gone away.
> *Espero que lleguen pronto ;* I hope they will arrive
> soon.

(3) It is used in temporal clauses referring to a future time.

> e.g., *Le hablaré cuando venga ;* I shall speak to him
> when he comes.

Mientras no llueva, escaseará el trigo ; As long as
  there is no rain, wheat will be scarce.
En cuanto lleguen tendré que marcharme ; As soon
  as they arrive I shall have to leave.

(4) It is used in clauses governed by the following conjunctions so long as a definite fact is not related : *aunque*, although ; *para que*, so that ; *sin que*, without ; *con tal que*, provided that, etc.

e.g., *Aunque sea rico no me comprará nada ;* Although
  he *may be* rich, he will not buy me anything.
Aunque es rico no me compra nada ; Although he *is*
  rich (fact) he doesn't buy me anything.
Salí sin que me viesen ; I went out without their
  seeing me.

(5) It is used in relative clauses which depend on a negative or indefinite antecedent.

e.g., *Busco una casa que tenga el jardín grande ;* I am
  looking for a house (indefinite) with a big garden.
*Mi hermano vive en una casa que tiene el jardín
  grande ;* My brother lives in a house (definite,
  because it is my brother's) which has a large
  garden.
Necesito un empleado (unknown) *que hable francés ;*
  I want a clerk who can speak French.
Tengo un empleado que habla francés ; I have a
  clerk (definite, he's mine) who speaks French.

(6) It is used in clauses depending on Impersonal Verbs so long as they do not indicate certainty.

e.g., *Es posible que puedan pagarlo ;* It is possible that
  they can pay for it.
Es cierto, evidente, que pueden pagarlo ; It is
  certain, evident, that they can pay for it.
¿ Es cierto que puedan pagarlo ? Is it certain
  (doubtful ?) that they can pay for it ?

> *Es preciso que muevan las patas de la mesa ;* It is
> necessary to move the legs of the table.

(7) It is used in past tenses only, in clauses depending on *si*
(meaning " if ") (e.g., as in English clauses such as, " If they
came . . .", " If they had come . . .", " If I were . . .",
etc.). The Imperfect and Conditional Subjunctive are prac-
tically interchangeable.

> e.g., *Si* $\left\{ \begin{array}{l} \textit{vinieran} \\ \textit{viniesen} \end{array} \right\}$ *los veríamos ;* If they $\left\{ \begin{array}{l} \text{were to come} \\ \text{came} \end{array} \right\}$
> we should see them.

> *Si* $\left\{ \begin{array}{l} \textit{hubieran} \\ \textit{hubiesen} \end{array} \right\}$ *venido, los habríamos visto ;* If they
> had come (but they did not) we should have seen
> them.

> *Si yo fuese rico, compraría un castillo en España ;*
> If I were rich (but I'm not !) I should buy a
> castle in Spain.

Radical-changing Verbs

Class I

This class contains those verbs whose infinitive ends in *-ar*
or *-er*. When stressed the radical vowel *e* becomes *ie*, and *o*
becomes *ue*.

The change occurs only in the Present Tenses (Indicative
and Subjunctive) and the Imperative (Familiar).

(*N.B.* The Subjunctive is, of course, used for the Polite
Imperative.)

> e.g., *pensar*, to think
>> Present Indicative : **pienso, piensas, piensa,** *pen-*
>> *samos, penséis,* **piensan**
>> Present Subjunctive : **piense, pienses, piense,** *pen-*
>> *semos, penséis,* **piensen**
>> Familiar Imperative : **piensa,** *pensad*
>> *contar*, to relate, to count

Present Indicative : **cuento, cuentas, cuenta,** *con-*
tamos, contáis, **cuentan**

Present Subjunctive : **cuente, cuentes, cuente,** *con-*
temos, contéis, **cuenten**

Familiar Imperative : **cuenta,** *contad*

volver, to return

Present Indicative : **vuelvo, vuelves, vuelve,** *vol-*
vemos, volvéis, **vuelven**

Present Subjunctive : **vuelva, vuelvas, vuelva,** *vol-*
vamos, volváis, **vuelvan**

Familiar Imperative : **vuelve,** *volved*

perder, to lose

Present Indicative : **pierdo, pierdes, pierde,** *per-*
demos, perdéis, **pierden**

Present Subjunctive : **pierda, pierdas, pierda,** *per-*
damos, perdáis, **pierdan**

Familiar Imperative : **pierde,** *perded*

A few other common verbs of this class are :

acordarse, to remember	*encontrar,* to find
acostarse, to lie down	*llover,* to rain
almorzar, to lunch	*mover(se),* to move
cerrar, to close	*querer,* to love (want)
comenzar, to begin	*rogar,* to request
costar, to cost	*sentarse,* to sit
despertar(se), to awake	*sonar,* to sound
empezar, to begin	*soñar,* to dream
encender, to light	*volar,* to fly
entender, to understand	

Class II

This class contains verbs ending in *-entir, -erir, -ertir,* and
also *morir,* to die, and *dormir,* to sleep. Stressed vowels *o* and
e become *ue* and *ie* as in Class I, but also *o* becomes *u* and *e*
becomes *i*.

These changes occur as in Class I in the Present Indicative,

Present Subjunctive and Familiar Imperative, and also in the Gerund, and in the third persons, singular and plural, of the Past Historic and hence in the Imperfect Subjunctive.

> e.g., *sentir*, to feel, to regret
>> Present Indicative : **siento, sientes, siente,** *sentimos, sentís,* **sienten**
>> Present Subjunctive : **sienta, sientas, sienta, sintamos, sintáis, sientan**
>> Familiar Imperative : **siente,** *sentid*
>> Gerund (Present Participle) : **sintiendo**
>> Past Historic : *sentí, sentiste,* **sintió,** *sentimos, sentisteis,* **sintieron**
>> Imperfect Subjunctive : **sintiera, sintieras, sintiera, sintiéramos, sintierais, sintieran,** or **sintiese, sintieses, sintiese, sintiésemos, sintieseis, sintiesen**
>>
>> *dormir*, to sleep
>> Present Indicative : **duermo, duermes, duerme,** *dormimos, dormís,* **duermen**
>> Present Subjunctive : **duerma, duermas, duerma, durmamos, durmáis, duerman**
>> Familiar Imperative : **duerme,** *dormid*
>> Gerund (Present Participle) : **durmiendo**
>> Past Historic : *dormí, dormiste,* **durmió,** *dormimos, dormisteis,* **durmieron**
>> Imperfect Subjunctive : **durmiera, durmieras, durmiera, durmiéramos, durmierais, durmieran,** or **durmiese, durmieses, durmiese, durmiésemos, durmieseis, durmiesen**

Other common verbs of this class are :

advertir, to warn	*hervir*, to boil
arrepentirse, to repent	*mentir*, to lie
diferir, to differ, to delay	*preferir*, to prefer
divertir(se), to amuse	*referir*, to refer, to tell
herir, to wound	

Class III

This class contains verbs ending in *-ebir, -edir, -egir, -eguir, -enchir, -endir, -eñir, -estir, -etir* and, also, *servir*. The only change is *e* into *i*.

This change occurs wherever there was a change in Class II.

> e.g., *pedir,* to ask for
> > Present Indicative : **pido, pides, pide,** *pedimos, pedís,* **piden**
> > Present Subjunctive : **pida, pidas, pida, pidamos, pidáis, pidan**
> > Familiar Imperative : **pide,** *pedid*
> > Gerund (Present Participle) : **pidiendo**
> > Past Historic : *pedí, pediste,* **pidió,** *pedimos, pedisteis,* **pidieron**
> > Imperfect Subjunctive : **pidiera, pidieras, pidiera, pidiéramos, pidierais, pidieran,** or **pidiese, pidieses, pidiese, pidiésemos, pidieseis, pidiesen**
>
> > *vestir,* to dress
> > Present Indicative : **visto, vistes, viste,** *vestimos, vestís,* **visten**
> > Present Subjunctive : **vista, vistas, vista, vistamos, vistáis, vistan**
> > Familiar Imperative : **viste,** *vestid*
> > Gerund (Present Participle) : **vistiendo**
> > Past Historic : *vestí, vestiste,* **vistió,** *vestimos, vestisteis,* **vistieron**
> > Imperfect Subjunctive : **vistiera, vistieras, vistiera, vistiéramos, vistierais, vistieran,** or **vistiese, vistieses, vistiese, vistiésemos, vistieseis, vistiesen**

Other common verbs of Class III are :

corregir, to correct	*reír,* to laugh
elegir, to elect	*reñir,* to quarrel
gemir, to groan	*repetir,* to repeat
medir, to measure	*seguir,* to follow
regir, to rule	*sonreír,* to smile

Haber and Tener

Both these verbs mean " to have ", but :

Haber is used :

(1) As an auxiliary verb.

e.g., *Hemos dormido* ; We have slept.

Han llegado ; They have arrived.

(2) In the impersonal forms *hay, había, habrá*, etc., meaning, "There is" (are), "there was" (were), "there will be", etc.

e.g., *Hay un hombre* ; There is a man.

Había muchos niños ; There were many children.

No hubo bajas ; There were no casualties.

Habrá una fiesta ; There will be a party.

Habría tormenta ; There would be a thunder storm.

Ha habido sequía todo el verano ; There has been a drought the whole summer.

Tener is used :

(1) As an ordinary transitive verb, meaning " to possess ", " to hold ", etc.

e.g., *Tengo dos hermanos* ; I have two brothers.

Tenemos una casa de campo ; We have a country house.

¿ Qué tiene él en la mano derecha ? What is he holding in the right hand ?

(2) With *que*, meaning " to have to ", " must ".

e.g., *Tengo que escribir una carta* ; I must write a letter.

Tenemos que salir ; We must leave.

Durante un mes tuvieron que trabajar un día sí y otro no ; During a month they had to work every other day.

Había habido muchas quejas ; There had been many com-complaints.

(3) In the impersonal forms *hay que, había que,* etc., with an infinitive, meaning "it is necessary", "it was necessary", etc.

e.g., *Hay que correr ;* It is necessary to run.
Había que correr ; It was necessary to run.

(4) With *de,* meaning "to have to".

e.g., *Hemos de trabajar ;* We have to work.
Han de jugar al fútbol ; They have to play football.

(3) With certain nouns to form idiomatic expressions.
tengo calor, I am hot
tiene frío, he is cold
tienen hambre, they are hungry
tienen sed, they are thirsty
tenemos miedo, we are afraid

Ser and Estar

According to the meaning it has to convey, the verb "to be" must usually be translated into Spanish either by *ser* or by *estar.*

Ser is used :

(1) With predicate nouns.
e.g., *¿ Qué es ésto ?* What is this ?
Es un libro ; It is a book.
Es una mesa ; It is a table.

Estar is used :

(1) To express position.
e.g., *¿ Dónde estamos ?* Where are we ?
Estamos en Londres ; We are in London.
El libro está en el cajón ; The book is in the drawer.

(2) With adjectives to express permanent qualities, i.e., character, origin, unchangeable possession.

> e.g., *¿ De qué color son sus ojos ?* What colour are his/her eyes ?
>
> *Este bailarín es español ;* This dancer is Spanish.
>
> *Este bailarín es de Sevilla ;* This dancer comes from Seville.
>
> *El niño es inteligente ;* The child is intelligent.

(2) With adjectives to express temporary, transitory qualities and state of health.

> e.g., *El pañuelo está limpio ;* The handkerchief is clean.
>
> *El café está caliente ahora ;* The coffee is hot now.
>
> *¿ Cómo está usted ?* How are you ?
>
> *Mi hermano no está bueno ;* My brother is not well.
>
> *Hoy estamos contentos ;* We feel happy to-day.
>
> *Están de pie ;* They are standing.

(3) With Past Participles to express real passive voice (usually a personal subject is essential).

> e.g., *Juanito fué atropellado por un autobús ;* Johnny was run over by a bus.

(3) With Past Participles to express a state resulting from previous action.

> e.g., *Estamos cansados por haber andado mucho ;* We are tired having walked so much.
>
> *Están sentados ;* They are sitting down (i.e., seated).
>
> *La ventana ha estado cerrada mucho tiempo ;* The window has been closed a long time.

COMMON IRREGULAR VERBS

P.G. = Pretérito Grave

Infinitive and Meaning.	Present Participle and Past Participle.	Present Indicative.	Present Subjunctive 1st Person Only.
andar to go, walk	andando andado	ando, andas, anda, andamos, andáis, andan	ande, etc.
caber to be able to be contained in	cabiendo cabido	QUEPO, cabes, cabe, cabemos, cabéis, caben	QUEPA, etc.
caer to fall	CAYENDO caído	CAIGO, caes, cae, caemos, caéis, caen	CAIGA, etc.
dar to give	dando dado	DOY, das, da, damos, dais, dan	DÉ, etc.
decir to say, tell	diciendo DICHO	DIGO, DICES, DICE, decimos, decís, DICEN	DIGA, etc.
estar to be	estando estado	ESTOY, estás, está, estamos, estáis, están	esté, etc.
haber to have	habiendo habido	HE, HAS, HA, HEMOS, habéis, HAN	HAYA, etc.
hacer to do, make	haciendo HECHO	HAGO, haces, hace, hacemos, hacéis, hacen	HAGA, etc.
ir to go	YENDO ido	VOY, VAS, VA, VAMOS, VAIS, VAN	VAYA, etc.
oír to hear	OYENDO oído	OIGO, OYES, OYE, oímos, oís, OYEN	OIGA, etc.
poder to be able	PUDIENDO podido	PUEDO, PUEDES, PUEDE, podemos, podéis, PUEDEN	PUEDA, etc.
poner to put	poniendo PUESTO	PONGO, pones, pone, ponemos, ponéis, ponen	PONGA, etc.
querer to wish, love	queriendo querido	QUIERO, QUIERES, QUIERE queremos, queréis, QUIEREN	QUIERA, etc.
saber to know	sabiendo sabido	SÉ, sabes, sabe, sabemos, sabéis, saben	SEPA, etc.
salir to go out	saliendo salido	SALGO, sales, sale, salimos, salís, salen	SALGA, etc.
ser to be	siendo sido	SOY, ERES, ES, SOMOS, SOIS, SON	SEA, etc.
tener to have	teniendo tenido	TENGO, TIENES, TIENE, tenemos, tenéis, TIENEN	TENGA, etc.
traer to bring	TRAYENDO traído	TRAIGO, traes, trae, traemos, traéis, traen	TRAIGA, etc.
valer to be worth	valiendo valido	VALGO, vales, vale, valemos, valéis, valen	VALGA, etc.
venir to come	VINIENDO venido	VENGO, VIENES, VIENE, venimos, venís, VIENEN	VENGA, etc.
ver to see	viendo VISTO	VEO, ves, ve, vemos, veis, ven	VEA, etc.

Past Historic (or Preterite).	Imperfect Subjunctive.	Future.	Notes.
ANDUVE, ANDUVISTE, ANDUVO, ANDUVIMOS, ANDUVISTEIS, ANDUVIERON (P.G.)	ANDUVIERA or ANDUVIESE, etc.	andaré. etc.	
CUPE, CUPISTE, CUPO, CUPIMOS, CUPISTEIS, CUPIERON (P.G.)	CUPIERA or CUPIESE, etc.	CABRÉ, etc.	
caí, caíste, CAYÓ, caímos, caísteis, CAYERON	CAYERA or CAYESE, etc.	caeré, etc.	
DÍ, DISTE, DIÓ, DIMOS, DISTEIS, DIERON	DIERA or DIESE, etc.	daré, etc.	
DIJE, DIJISTE, DIJO, DIJIMOS, DIJISTEIS, DIJERON (P.G.)	DIJERA or DIJESE, etc.	DIRÉ, etc.	
ESTUVE, ESTUVISTE, ESTUVO, ESTUVIMOS, ESTUVISTEIS, ESTUVIERON (P.G.)	ESTUVIERA or ESTUVIESE, etc.	estaré, etc.	
HUBE, HUBISTE, HUBO, HUBIMOS, HUBISTEIS, HUBIERON (P.G.)	HUBIERA or HUBIESE, etc.	HABRÉ, etc.	
HICE, HICISTE, HIZO, HICIMOS, HICISTEIS, HICIERON (P.G.)	HICIERA or HICIESE, etc.	HARÉ, etc.	
FUÍ, FUISTE, FUÉ, FUIMOS, FUISTEIS, FUERON	FUERA or FUESE, etc.	iré, etc.	*Imperfect* IBA
oí, oíste, OYÓ, oímos, oísteis, OYERON	OYERA or OYESE, etc.	oiré, etc.	
PUDE, PUDISTE, PUDO, PUDIMOS, PUDISTEIS, PUDIERON (P.G.)	PUDIERA or PUDIESE, etc.	PODRÉ, etc.	
PUSE, PUSISTE, PUSO, PUSIMOS, PUSISTEIS, PUSIERON (P.G.)	PUSIERA or PUSIESE, etc.	PONDRÉ, etc.	
QUISE, QUISISTE, QUISO, QUISIMOS, QUISISTEIS, QUISIERON (P.G.)	QUISIERA or QUISIESE, etc.	QUERRÉ, etc.	
SUPE, SUPISTE, SUPO, SUPIMOS, SUPISTEIS, SUPIERON (P.G.)	SUPIERA or SUPIESE, etc.	SABRÉ, etc.	
salí, saliste, salió, salimos salisteis, salieron	saliera or saliese, etc.	SALDRÉ, etc.	
FUÍ, FUISTE, FUÉ, FUIMOS, FUISTEIS, FUERON	FUERA or FUESE, etc.	seré, etc.	*Imperfect* ERA
TUVE, TUVISTE, TUVO, TUVIMOS, TUVISTEIS, TUVIERON (P.G.)	TUVIERA or TUVIESE, etc.	TENDRÉ, etc.	
TRAJE, TRAJISTE, TRAJO, TRAJIMOS, TRAJISTEIS, TRAJERON (P.G.)	TRAJERA or TRAJESE, etc.	traeré, etc.	
valí, valiste, valió, valimos, valísteis, valieron	valiera or valiese, etc.	VALDRÉ, etc.	
VINE, VINISTE, VINO, VINIMOS, VINISTEIS, VINIERON (P.G.)	VINIERA or VINIESE, etc.	VENDRÉ, etc.	
ví, viste, vió, vimos, visteis, vieron	viera or viese, etc.	veré, etc.	*Imperfect* VEÍA